The Art of

Civilized
Conversation

The Art of
Civilized
Conversation

A Guide to Expressing Yourself
with Style and Grace

● ● ●

Margaret Shepherd

with Sharon Hogan

Illustrations by Penny Carter

BROADWAY BOOKS

New York

Broadway Books titles may be purchased for business or promotional use or for special sales. For information, please write to: Special Markets Department, Random House, Inc., 1745 Broadway, New York, NY 10019.

PRINTED IN THE UNITED STATES OF AMERICA

BROADWAY BOOKS and its logo, a letter B bisected on the diagonal, are trademarks of Random House, Inc.

Visit our Web site at www.broadwaybooks.com

First edition published 2006

Book design by rlf design

Library of Congress Cataloging-in-Publication Data
Shepherd, Margaret.
    The art of civilized conversation : a guide to expressing yourself with
style and grace / Margaret Shepherd with Sharon Hogan.— 1st ed.
        p.   cm.
    Includes bibliographical references.
    1. Conversation.   I. Hogan, Sharon.   II. Title.

BJ2121.S48 2005
395.5'9—dc22

                                                            2005047212

ISBN 0-7679-2169-0

10 9 8 7 6 5 4 3 2 1

Contents

Acknowledgments

This book could not have been written without the conversations I shared with many of my favorite people. I want to thank them here.

First, I owe a debt of gratitude to Sharon Cloud Hogan, Colleen Mohyde, and Trish Dalton Medved, the kind of coauthor, agent, and editor that every writer dreams of.

I am grateful to other people who gave their time generously:

Ken Morse, who fosters civility every day at MIT. Marilyn Brandt, Jeanne Lauer Williams, and Lilian Kemp, for their enduring friendship and interest. David Friend, Zoe Friend, Lily Friend, Miriam Friend, Geoffrey Shepherd, Gordon Shepherd, Sherman Lewis, and Tom, Kiernan, and Liam Hogan, for their family support.

Sophia Ainslee and Lauran Niegos of Crane's Paper Company, and Michael McCurdy, Bob Lauer, Stephanie Loo, Vimala Rodgers, and Nancy Mairs, for their expert advice and personal testimony. The reference staff at the Boston Public Library for their help in tracking down citations. Lindsay McGrath, Leonie Luterman, and Ruth Owen, for their special wisdom as hospital chaplains. Jeanne Wei, MD, and Erlene Rosowsky, PsyD, for their insights into talking with older adults. Elizabeth Willingham, for her words of wisdom on family dynamics. Ann Densmore, EdD, for her advice on talking with children.

And thank you to all other friends, relations, colleagues, and bystanders—both willing and unaware—who talked and listened while this book took shape.

The Art of
Civilized
Conversation

Introduction

ONE PERSON walks into a café, sits down to a cup of coffee in silence, finishes it, and goes back to the same old day. Two other people walk into that café, sit down to two cups of coffee, have a good talk—and go on their way with fresh energy, comfort, and insight. Simply by connecting them, conversation has changed them. And that's the definition of art. Civilized conversation is an art that transforms everyday life into something richer. It can engage your mind, excite your imagination, and expand your view of the world.

Just as a civilized conversation can get the morning off to a great start, it can enhance your work life all through the day and invigorate an evening of social life. If you enjoy the art of conversation with your family and friends, you will also shine at breakfast with a client, lunch with coworkers, and dinner with your boss. It's the Swiss Army knife of social skills that anyone can learn to use. Take it with you wherever you go, and you'll be equipped to turn a seatmate into a confidant, an interviewer into an employer, and an acquaintance into a friend. As an accomplished conversationalist, you'll be welcomed everywhere; everyone loves good conversation because it is *fun*.

Conversation, which is a craft as well as an art, requires only a little talent and a lot of practice. You don't have to be Michelangelo, just a good mechanic. The more you practice, the better you get and the more pleasure it brings. Anyone can refine the art of civilized conversation with virtually anyone else, regardless of dissimilarities in age, status, job, family, or abilities. Good talking skills can help you bridge distances and differences of opinion with people you want to stay close to. If you're new in town or starting a new phase of life, it can smooth the transition. Whether you are beginning to speak English or learning to use it better, the art of conversation will help you with exactly which words to say and when.

This book will help you excel at conversation. It will show you how to talk and listen better—and find more pleasure in doing both. It holds dozens of helpful ideas that will sweeten, smooth, and strengthen your social life so you can look forward to your day—from the first "good morning" to the reflections you share over an evening meal. If you usually fear that you will bungle an introduction at a party, this book will provide you with enough opening lines to knit a safety net. These suggestions will help you enjoy meaningful exchanges—not just fulfill social obligations. They will help you delight in social repartee—not just survive it. By the time you reach the last page of this book, you will be the kind of sparkling conversationalist who also makes other people shine.

What Civilized Conversation Is and Is Not

Where I grew up in the Midwest, when you get together with someone, you don't just *talk*; that would be commonplace. Nor do you *converse*; that would be pretentious. Instead, you *visit*. You can visit on the phone and visit on the street. "Let's just visit with each other awhile" means that you welcome each other to a space you've created just by talking. Conversation doesn't get much better than that.

Conversation lets you be an artist every time you open your mouth—or shut it. As Robert Louis Stevenson said, "The most important art is to omit"; the key to being a master conversationalist is to listen at least as much as you talk. Just as the other arts include pauses in a dramatic play, white margins around printed text, and space between a singer's phrases, conversation is about silences as well as about words.

In addition to listening well, the other simple principles of civilized conversation—don't ramble, don't gossip, don't bore, and disagree carefully—are not arbitrary demands of etiquette; rather, they are based on caring about yourself and about others. Etiquette and manners are not out-of-date rules. Instead, they are generally accepted guidelines for making everyone comfortable enough to connect.

Good conversation is classy, humane, practical, universal, and, when well done, seemingly effortless. It can also be defined by what it is *not*—civilized conversation is not the same as reciting, confessing, negotiating, scolding, or interviewing. It does not involve notifying, debating, or issuing orders, nor does it include baiting, shouting, hurling personal insults, contradicting, grandstanding, or interrupting. It does not require a referee. It is most surely *not* what people hear on many television and radio talk shows: that is performance art of particular emptiness, and the worst example of how to converse.

Good conversation rarely occurs when one party is not paying reasonable attention. In fact, courtesy is crucial to the very existence of a civilized exchange. By that I don't mean that you must always trot out the proper protocol or the perfect words, but you must connect somehow with the other person. Conversation is much less dignified if one person is phoning, instant messaging, e-mailing, reading, watching television, wearing headphones, humming, or staring into space. Your actions reveal to the other person exactly what you consider most important. Your concentration on other tasks can dilute the conversation, especially if you are not making eye contact with the person with whom you are talking.

Civilized conversation can take place, however, while you are riding in a car, listening to some background music, playing cards or a board game, golfing, gardening, hiking, doing dishes, or sitting in a hot tub; the conversation is often just less intense. Some people find it easier to relax if they are doing something unimportant while they talk, or if they sit side by side when eye contact may seem too intimate. These settings are fine—as long as the other person knows that you are really focusing on him or her. In fact, some of the very best talk happens when people are sitting around a table and savoring a good meal.

How to Use This Book

Conversation is a big part of human life, and this book doesn't cover every aspect of it. Families have their own private language, tailored to their unique needs. In this book, you will not find tips for your own in-house talk, nor will you find advice about child rearing or how to save your marriage. You'll also have to look elsewhere if you're searching for quips to liven your next speech or tips to make better sales calls. This book is about how to enjoy civilized conversation.

The Art of Civilized Conversation can improve your social conversations, regardless of your insecurities or inexperience. You may dread facing a room full of strangers at networking cocktail parties. Your mind may go numb when you try to retrieve people's names from your memory bank. You may gulp and stammer when you introduce yourself, grope for the right words at weddings, and struggle through small talk with casual acquaintances or serious talk with someone who means a great deal to you. If you make blunders even when you mean well, relax and keep reading. This book will walk you through what to say and what not to say in all the classic situations. You will acquire the conversational know-how to handle almost any eventuality, and soon you will welcome rather than shrink from every encounter. Whether you read this book cover to cover or skim it for specific advice, you will find again and again that it helps you to put the confidence back into your conversations.

A conversation distinguishes humans from animals. It lies at the very core of who we are. It is one of the first capacities to develop in infancy, and each person's unique conversational style becomes part of his or her personality for a lifetime. A standard nursery school rule can civilize anyone's life: "Use words." In this book, I have distilled my experience with using words—the awesome and the awful, the gaffes I have made and the ones I have forgiven, and the many heartening moments when I felt really connected with the people I cared about. I hope that these home truths will encourage you to use your own words with graciousness and care—and that they will give you new insight into what makes people tick when they talk.

· I ·

What Conversations
Are Made Of

Sweet discourse, the banquet of the mind.
—John Dryden, *Fables Ancient and Modern,* 1700

O NLY CONNECT!" In the novel *Howard's End*, E. M. Forster considered what it would mean to "live in fragments no longer." A century later, in an even more fragmented world, you may have only a few minutes to connect with someone new or reconnect with a friend. You can make the most of these happy opportunities by knowing what goes into good conversation. Whether you're aware of it or not, you already have the rich resources that you need to converse well. You simply have to tap in to them.

Tools of the Trade: Your Voice, Face, and Body

Every expressive art begins with a set of tools. In the art of conversation, you are both the artist and the tool kit. Though some things about you can't be changed, you can learn to make the best use of your voice, facial expressions, body, and body language. Most people will respond to the things about you that you have chosen, like your smile, your posture, and your clothes. The people who are worth talking to will not focus on the things you can't change, like your height, your face, and your race.

How You Sound

Your tone of voice and facial expressions are much more important than how pretty or stylish you look. Many of the nicest words don't work if the tone is wrong, whereas many awkward phrases will be forgiven if you smile and speak pleasantly. Sometimes the difference between a minor blooper and a real insult is the speaker's intonation and the look on his face. For instance, "congratulations" means one thing if enunciated with a low-pitched voice through gritted teeth, quite another if pitched higher with a sincere smile. Go one octave higher, however, and you will ring insincere. "You deserve each other" is an insult in an ironic tone and a compliment in a caring one. In the movie *Donnie Brasco,* actor Johnny Depp uses tone of voice to give at least half a dozen different meanings to the phrase "forgetaboutit."

Likewise, take care to put the emphasis on words so that you mean what you say. For instance, a friend who shows up late will hear a different message depending on where you place the emphasis in: *Where* have you been? Where *have* you been? Where have *you* been? Where have you *been*?

Pay attention to how loud you speak, and be willing to change your volume when you need to. Notice whether people are backing off and bracing themselves for the blast, or leaning in and straining to hear.

If you mumble, you risk not only being misunderstood, but frustrating your audience as well. Never drop your voice to a breathy whisper in an effort to get people to pay closer attention to you. That may have worked for Marilyn Monroe, but if you want to be taken seriously, speak up.

How You Look

Be pretty if you can, witty if you must, and pleasant if it kills you.
—Laura Ingalls Wilder, *Little Town on the Prairie,* 1953

When Prince Charles was introduced to the actress Susan Hampshire in 1973, she was wearing a very low-cut dress. He said to her, "Father told me that if I ever meet a young lady in a dress like yours, I must look her straight in the eye." People will enjoy conversing with you more if they are not distracted by what you're wearing. Do your homework. If you're going to a party, check the dress code. If you think you need a shower, you probably do. If high heels make you feel that you loom over people, wear flats. If people don't treat you seriously, dress like a grown-up! If you want your own Prince Charming to remember your face, cover up the rest a bit. Don't be afraid to present the real you—not more, not less.

Although you don't want to offend people, there's no need to be completely neutral in how you dress. You don't need to keep your profile too low. In fact, if what you wear gives clues to who you are, you will appeal to like-minded people. Express yourself with a conversation piece like a ring, a piece of antique jewelry, or another accessory item. I have a very funny-looking purse of red fur, designed for me by my daughter at age fourteen. It's comfortable to carry and easy to keep track of, and as a conversation piece it really works. At a recent fundraising party for a dance group, a total stranger rushed up to me with a smile on her face. "You're the lady with the purse! I saw you last month in the post office and a week later I saw you at the book fair, and now here you are!" This coincidence, which was not particularly meaningful to anyone but her, was enough to introduce us to each other, and our common interest in the dance group then led to a very lively conversation.

Before you arrive anywhere, tuck in your shirt, smooth down your hair, and check your teeth for spinach. If you clean up, dress with care, stand up straight, smile, and make eye contact, you're already on your way to making others more comfortable and receptive. Your self-confidence that you look appealing will *make* you appeal to people.

How You Move

When you meet new people or go to another country, don't assume that others share your customs for handshaking, touching, and allowing personal space. Be sensitive to how people are reacting and to the ways in which your motions may be misinterpreted. A good rule of thumb is to keep an arm's length of distance between yourself and the person with whom you are speaking. Don't throw yourself at people who are not "huggers" or recoil if a kisser tries to plant one on you—or laugh if they give you two or three kisses on the cheek or in the air.

Finally, while you tone down your own distracting habits, try to forgive them in others—if someone's accent puts you off, try to listen through it; if someone doesn't make eye contact, try to establish some other kind of connection. Forgive as you would like to be forgiven.

Once you're comfortable with the physical tools that can make you a confident artist in conversation, you can consider how to transform everyday words into something extraordinary. Conversation has a basic format that anyone can learn. The following suggestions will help you begin, shape, and end a good conversation and fix its most common problems.

Greetings and Introductions

All conversations begin before words are exchanged. The energy that you convey when you enter a room—or when another person does—can set the tone. At an absolute minimum, face the other person, look into his or her eyes, and show evidence of goodwill and respect. Smile, but don't bare your teeth.

When you make a new acquaintance, start off with your best manners. You can always ease into informality as you get to know each other, but it's awkward to retreat into formality. Once you've said "Hey, Mandy, how's it going?" it's difficult to go back to a more reserved "Hello, Mrs. Delacourt."

Practice old-fashioned courtesy: stand up, especially if you are a man, if you are younger than the other person, or if you have less status. When you're introduced, use the person's title and last name (e.g., Mr. O'Brien) until you are invited to be on a first-name basis, particularly with older people.

Remember to set an appropriate physical distance. Get down to the eye level of a child or a wheelchair user. Speak at an audible but not overpowering volume, and take turns speaking. Don't interrupt or contradict except to correct someone who gets your name wrong. Now you're off on the right foot.

How to Say Hello

Dolly: Hello! Hello there, how are you? Oh Hello!
Horace: You know too many people.
Dolly: Total strangers!
Horace: Then why do you greet them?
Dolly: It makes me feel good to have so many friends.
Horace: Oh, say hello for me too then.

Dolly: I already did.
—From the film *Hello Dolly,* 1969

When you greet someone, smile as you address him or her.

You might say:

➤ How do you do?; Hello.

➤ Pleased to make your acquaintance; Pleased to meet you.

➤ Good morning; Good afternoon; (and maybe) Good evening.

➤ Happy holidays.

➤ It's good to see you; It's good to meet you.

Don't say:

➤ Hey, you over there . . . ; Hey, handsome; 'Sup?; S'happening?; Yo!

➤ I'm so excited to meet you; I can't believe I'm talking to you! (These greetings force the other person to respond with either false modesty or fatuousness.)

➤ Remember me?

How to Introduce Yourself

Dr. Livingstone, I presume?
—Sir Henry Morton Stanley, *How I Found Livingstone,* 1871

To introduce yourself to a new person, you can start with "Hello. My name is Sally" or "I'm Sally (or Sally Suave)" or "I'd like to introduce myself. I'm Sally." In a group, a handshake plus your name is acceptable.

People you don't know are not a big, amorphous crowd of strangers. Although in a group they may seem like an imposing solid brick wall, it may be better to think of a crowd as a wall of individual windows that can each offer you a different view of life. If you follow the many tips and small strategies contained in this book, even self-introduction can be a pleasure.

When you introduce yourself by saying your own name, don't use your title. Even if other people call you Mrs. Murray, introduce yourself as Eleanor Murray or Eleanor. However, with children who need help knowing what to call you, you can introduce yourself as Aunt Eleanor or Grandma Ellie if you want them to call you that.

A teacher introduces himself to his students with the title he would like them to use—Mr. Goodge or Dr. Goodge—but writes his whole name on the board: George Goodge. In intellectual circles, an inverse snobbery restrains professors from injecting their titles into introductions ("Hello, I'm Fred Mayhem"), though others may add them ("Hello, Dr. Mayhem.")

You will be on safe ground if you address both current and retired military, ambassadorial, clerical, and judicial people by their profession (Colonel Smith, Ambassador Smith, Reverend Smith, Father Smith, Justice Smith) or simply as "sir" or "ma'am" until you are very sure of protocol in their worlds. When in doubt, ask. Aristocratic titles may call for a quick check of the etiquette books.

After you have said hello and your name, you may wish to expand on your introduction with pleasantries such as "Good to see you," "Nice to meet you," or "Nice to see you again."

If another person is introducing you, just make eye contact and offer to shake hands when you are being introduced. If your introducer has mangled your name, say it again clearly for your new acquaintance.

If you aren't clear of the other person's name, as you say something along the lines of "Nice to meet you," say the name again with an inquiring expression to let him or her correct what you think you heard. If you want to start right in on a first-name basis, just repeat your first name.

Once the other person has introduced himself, use the person's title and last name (e.g., Mr. Smith) until you are invited to be on a first-name basis.

TO REINTRODUCE YOURSELF to a brief former acquaintance (if you do not remember the person's name), say "Hello. My name is _____ ." Then the person will most likely respond with his or her name. If not, you can say "I remember you, but I've forgotten your name," or "You may not remember me; I'm Rafik." Always reintroduce yourself to young children who may have forgotten which one of the grown-ups you are in the interval since they saw you last.

IF YOU WISH to introduce yourself to someone who is of greater status or age, simply use good manners: "Good morning, sir. My name is Matt Frieberg; I'm your wife's student."

If you are the person with higher status, pay attention to the person who has made the effort to introduce himself to you. You, too, should use your best manners and be civilized. Don't let a seemingly unimportant person turn you into a snob. My English-born father often told of a conversation he'd overheard: A humble young academic who was visiting a hidebound English university skirted protocol and had the gall to introduce himself to a professor at a gathering (rather than wait for a mutual friend to introduce them). "Good afternoon, sir, my name is Eric Kincaid," he said as he extended his hand. "Oh, really?" drawled the older man in his best upper-crust Etonian voice, and then he turned away.

How to Remember Names

A gifted conversationalist seems to remember every name, every time. With a little help and some practice, you can too.

1. Gather your wits before you meet a new group of people. If you can, do your homework ahead of time with a list of names that you will then connect to faces.

2. When you are introduced, pay attention to the other person's name. Say it out loud as you make eye contact, say it at least once during the conversation, and say it again when you part.

3. Say the name over a few times in your mind and link it to a visual image: if her name is Mary Jane, imagine her wearing Mary Jane shoes. Or connect the person with others who have that name; visualize the Ben Lincoln you've just met standing next to Abe Lincoln.

4. Use rhyming: "Tall Paul" or "Nate the waiter." (Just don't say it out loud.)

5. Follow up. Reinforce your memory by looking at his name tag, asking him for a card, and writing his name down as soon as you get home.

A truly great human being does not commit cruelty by being uncivil to a person with lesser status. Give everyone you chance to meet at least three minutes of your time and attention. Be kind.

How to Introduce Others

A senator once took Will Rogers to the White House to meet President Coolidge. Inside the Oval Office, the senator introduced the two men. "Will Rogers," he said, "I'd like you to meet President Coolidge."

Deadpan, Rogers quipped, "I'm sorry, but I didn't catch the name."

—Steve Goodier, *Joy Along the Way*, 2002

Another way to initiate a courteous conversation is to be attentive to occasions when introductions are in order. When you find yourself in a group of people who require introductions, first say the name of the woman, the older person, or the higher-ranking person. Repeat this rule over and over, and rehearse it with a friend if it is a stumbling point: *the lady, the elder, or the honored person comes first.* For example:

> ➤ Mom, this is my friend Matt Chang. Matt, this is my mother, Lynda Weber. (Matt's response will be "Hello, Mrs. [or Ms.] Weber" or "Hello, Lynda [if you said only her first name].)

> ➤ Governor Kelley, I'd like you to meet Tony Buck. Tony, this is Governor Kelley.

> ➤ Senator, may I present my assistant, Elizabeth Valdez? Elizabeth, this is Senator Claghorn. (Ms. Valdez then says "Hello, Senator Claghorn" and can call him "Senator" or "Senator Claghorn" for the rest of the evening.)

Once you've made the first introduction, say it again in reverse order. If the two individuals seem evenly matched in status, you can say, "I'd like you two to meet," and start the introduction with either person. Name order may seem like a hair-splitting, nitpicking, illogical point of etiquette, and in some circles these niceties will pass unnoticed, but in other settings people will value your attention to manners. And *somebody's* name has to be first! Why not practice doing it correctly?

Do your homework if you think you may be meeting people with titles other than Mr., Mrs., Miss, and Ms. Listen carefully to how other people use titles as other introductions are being made. When in doubt, combine logic and respect, and welcome clarification. If you don't know a person's exact title, ask, or at least leave an opening for him or her to correct you: "Reverend Scott, I'd like you to meet my sister, Jeanne Mudge. Is it 'reverend,' or do you prefer 'doctor'?" "Jeanne, this is Dr. Scott." (Jeanne should then call him Dr. Scott, not Doctor.)

Stay alert for appropriate ways to use even common titles such as Mrs. and ma'am. When used on their own (not before names), these titles may convey something that you didn't mean at all. An older woman may relish being called "miss" or she may prefer "ma'am." "Sir" may make a middle-aged man feel like an elder statesman or a geezer in a rocker. "Lady" sounds offhand when you use it alone, as in "Let me tell you, lady, that's the firm price." Use "ma'am" instead. "Young lady" may flatter a child, but your own daughter may not like it in the question "Where have you *been,* young lady?"

Likewise, if a husband and wife have different last names, try to remember both of them. Don't automatically "Mrs." a "Ms." Don't take it upon yourself to question her reasons for not taking her husband's name or slap a conventional label over her own.

SOMETIMES YOUR MIND goes blank while you are introducing people, or you cannot place the person you are talking to. The face is vaguely familiar and the person acts like he knows you, but the name and story escape your memory. When struck with a case of total nonrecall,

Do:

➢ Admit a memory lapse and ask for help. "Who are you? We've met before." "I remember you, but I don't remember your name." "I'm drawing a blank on your name." "I should remember where we met. . . ." "I am [name] and we know each other. . . ." "We are both friends of Sam's." Once you've admitted your memory lapse, don't elaborate! As soon as the other person reminds you what his name is, quickly move on.

➢ Pull a third person into the conversation and present him to your unnamed friend ("Let me introduce you to my friend Pedro"). The person whose name you can't remember will then have to introduce himself to Pedro. If he doesn't jump in, you have another chance to ask his name. This lame option is not the best manners, but at least you'll get another opportunity. Pay attention this time.

➢ If you're over fifty, you may start to get a free pass on memory lapses—not flattering, but merciful. "I'm having a senior moment here. . . ."

➢ Write the person's name down, explaining that you have trouble with names and really want to get it right so that you can keep in touch.

➢ Offer the person your business card and hope he reciprocates.

Don't:

➤ Risk using the wrong name.

➤ Apologize repeatedly, calling strident attention to how forgettable the person is.

If another person appears to be struggling to retrieve your name from his memory bank, come to his rescue. Again, correct the person, gently but promptly, if he mispronounces your name.

To introduce one person to a crowd of several people, make a general introduction. For instance, "Hello, everyone, this is Joyce Johnson, our new neighbor. Joyce, these are the poker players I was telling you about. Mike, would you introduce Joyce around to a few people while I get her a drink?"

If you are Mike, introduce Joyce to at least three people so that she will feel comfortable mingling after she has finished her first conversation about Texas hold 'em.

Once you've helped other people to identify each other with a name, provide them with some common links to launch their own conversation (e.g., "Mom, this is José. We went to camp together"). Don't, however, follow the introduction with a long recitation of the person's résumé—that implies that he or she is not interesting enough in person but needs extra puffing up to be worth talking to. You also risk imposing your own issues and priorities onto other people's first impressions. Say "Janice has years of experience in teaching watercolor painting" rather than "Janice is the world's greatest watercolor artist." Or "Adam just had a guest appearance on the WPDQ comedy hour" rather than "Adam tells the greatest jokes. C'mon, Adam, tell one now!"

After you've made the introduction, step back and let the new acquaintances get to know one another. Don't continue to dominate the exchange. A man I know named Frank, who worked part-time as a driver's education teacher, had mixed feelings about his wife's success as a research chemist. He developed a habit of showcasing her when they were with friends: "Lena, tell everyone about the amazing discovery Perrione Labs made last year." Then, when she started to describe it, he would interrupt with "Yes, but that's not the part you told me about," and he would continue coaching her to try to impress the listeners with his involvement, however peripheral.

It's important to suggest connections between people who have just met, but don't order them to pursue these links, especially if you have only provided a dead-end, boring conversational lead-in. "You were both at the same school" is better than "Tell each other about how you blacked out at a frat party." An opening line like the following, from the movie *Bridget Jones's Diary*, is an absolute nonstarter: "Natasha, this is Bridget Jones. Bridget works in a publishing house and she used to play around naked in my paddling pool."

YOU CAN connect people with each other if you get your mouth connected to your brain. Here's a poorly thought-out introduction:

Hello, Joe. There you are. I'd like you to meet my friend Don. We knew each other in school—what was it, Don? Through the debating club or the yearbook? All I know is we used to argue all the time—and then, just last January, he turned up at a convention where my wife was giving a talk, and we couldn't believe the coincidence after all those years! We were just amazed. Don, this is Joe.

You've just overwhelmed Joe with a lot of vague, useless information about the connection between you and Don and minimized Joe by giving no information at all. You haven't given them anything useful to get a conversation and acquaintance started. Try again:

Hello, Joe. It's good to see you. This is my old friend from high school, Don. Don, this is Joe. He's a talented photographer like you. You have a lot in common, plus you both married into big families.

Now you can just enjoy watching your two friends get acquainted, and maybe learn something new about them yourself.

Joining a Conversation

Sir, I look upon every day to be lost, in which I do not make a new acquaintance.

—Samuel Johnson, quoted in *Boswell's Life of Johnson,* 1744

Many people fear certain conversational settings that tie their stomachs in knots beforehand and send them home afterward convinced they can't connect with others. If you get those knots, too, go prepared with some of these tactics already in mind.

Let's say, for instance, that you're at a stand-up cocktail party. Everyone is chatting happily. You don't know anyone. To avoid this scenario completely, veteran cocktail partygoers start with a good offense—they go early and appear to welcome each new arrival as if they were part of the established group. Other savvy socializers use the preemptive tactic of going with a buddy. That way, after they've split up and made a few self-introductions, they can share with each other the interesting people each has met. If you're by yourself, here are your main options:

> ➢ Stand around. Others may see that you're on your own, or someone may recognize you and approach you.

> ➢ Sit down. You may be able to strike up a conversation with another guest who is sitting down.

➤ Walk around. Roaming temporarily camouflages your solitary state, but doesn't solve it.

➤ Look for another wallflower. Most crowds contain more than one. Greet another wallflower with "How do you know [the host]?" "I don't know many people here, do you?" or "I'm glad to meet someone." Once you've rescued each other, you can approach a group of other guests as a team.

➤ Seek help from or offer help to the host. Don't dominate the host's time or distract him from other duties, but when he is available, it's okay to ask for a couple of introductions. You may also offer to pass appetizers around to break the ice (but don't go help in the kitchen unless other guests are there too).

➤ Try to enter a conversation. You may find a congenial person who welcomes you. You might say "I'm new here. May I introduce myself?" or "I just got here. Could I join your conversation? My name is_____ " or simply "Hello."

➤ Make eye contact. People will think they know you.

➤ Stand by the food. It's a topic you will have in common with everyone who approaches the table.

Whether you've been introduced to another person or you've introduced yourself, once you've struck up a conversation, keep going. You can employ many creative twists on customary pleasantries to go beyond "How are you?" "I'm fine, thank you, how are you?" To equip yourself with some ways to jump-start new conversations, read on.

Opening Lines and Small Talk

"The time has come," the Walrus said,
"To talk of many things:
Of shoes—and ships—and sealing wax—
Of cabbages—and Kings—
And why the sea is boiling hot—
And whether pigs have wings."
—Lewis Carroll, *Through the Looking Glass,* 1872

One of my favorite Chinese proverbs is "There are three hundred and forty-six subjects for elegant conversation." Although you need not commit 346 subjects to memory, there are lots of things to talk about, even with the newest acquaintance. It's helpful to keep some of them in mind when you need an icebreaker. If you are passionate about a particular interest—fly-fishing, growing violets or orchids, or collecting rare books or minerals—and if you can convey your enthusiasm for your hobby in a way that allows people to talk about theirs, you are already well on your way to being a fascinating conversationalist.

Lots of people have unexpected interests, and almost everybody collects something or knows someone who does. Ask what he or she likes to collect. You may discover that you share a traditional hobby, like collecting old coins, or a more obscure one, like collecting first-edition copies of books by Tolstoy.

Current affairs such as a news item that's likely to have been seen by others, recent poll results, or interesting discoveries or inventions also provide good starting points for conversation.

Conversation Kindling: Rub Two Clichés Together to Spark a Dialogue

Consider this trick for making your opening lines electrifying and elegant. Take two seemingly unrelated ideas and shake them up for a fresh twist on an old opener:

- "Cold enough for you?" and "Nice coat" equals: "That's a beautiful color you've got on; it warms me up just to look at it!"

- "I'm so tired" plus "What about those Yankees?" equals: "Watching the World Series is like having a second job. Are you following the games?"

- "You look good" plus "Nice jacket" equals: "You look like an athlete. Is that a team insignia?"

- "How's the family?" plus "Long time no see" equals: "I wonder what music (or ideas, sports, or technology) your kids are into now that they are teenagers. I feel like I'm one lap behind here."

- "Gee, you've grown" plus "Still reading all those comic books?" equals: "I haven't seen you for two years. You must have grown into some new interests that I need to catch up on."

The Old Standbys

Once in a while, fascinating opening lines don't come to mind, and you have to fall back on an old classic opener when you're making someone's acquaintance. In some awkward situations, these comfortable standbys are fine. Because they are so common, you can avoid putting someone off by getting too personal right away. Here are some lines to draw from. When you have to use one, opt for the sparkling version over the desperate one:

> ➤ SPARKLING: All this sun for January! If you close your eyes it feels like Miami, not Buffalo!/Have you gotten out to enjoy this nice weather?/Do you enjoy the winters here, or would you prefer to be somewhere else?
>
> DESPERATE: Nice weather!

> ➤ SPARKLING: Do you have anything special planned for the holidays?/Long weekend?/Summer break?
>
> DESPERATE: Working hard, or hardly working?

> ➤ SPARKLING: My grandmother used to make baklava just like this. Do you do much cooking?
>
> DESPERATE: Would you look at all of this food! I'm going to go off my diet.

Small-Talk Saboteurs

Great opening lines can lead to rich conversations. Poor opening lines can be a conversational kiss of death. So can phrases or statements that offend, irritate, or otherwise put a damper on one's dialogue.

Shakespeare said, "Things without all remedy should be without remark." If you want to be successful at small talk, steer clear of negative pronouncements in general and any moping, self-pitying remarks that seem to whine "It had to be me." These include phrases about your aches and pains and about how mad you are about some current issue:

- ➤ I'm so upset.
- ➤ You know what I really hate? You know what really makes me mad?
- ➤ I don't know what this generation is coming to . . .
- ➤ I can't believe . . . [when it is overly dramatic and full of insignificant contradiction]
- ➤ They say . . . ; I'll tell you what . . . ; As I always say . . .

Also, avoid launching into a discussion of your own foibles and petty economies. For instance, people probably don't care about the particulars of why you're late, or how your dress is held together with a safety pin. One short anecdote is enough; let others chime in if they're interested or move on if not.

Ditto pets. Unless you know that the person you are speaking with has a dog (and you probably don't if you just met him), he probably isn't interested in how many rolls of Life Savers your beagle consumed and regurgitated last night. If you begin with this sort of anecdote, make it short and dramatic, and leave something to the imagination. Spare your listeners the fine details of the expensive canine X-rays that ensued.

Always check your audience before you proceed. Every few minutes, look for signs of polite boredom: glazed expressions, loss of eye contact, or listeners who are silently drifting away. Be prepared to share the floor with other dog owners who want to tell their own battle stories.

Likewise, unless you are talking with a professional shopper or a real estate agent, your listener probably isn't fascinated by things you've bought, bargains you got, and how much more your house is worth now than when you bought it. Everyone knows that college tuition is expensive. Why dwell on it?

Finally, try not to utter self-absorbed comments like:

> ➤ I had the strangest dream. You were in it. Uh, let me try to remember it. . . .

> ➤ You remind me of someone. You look just like . . .

> ➤ Want to hear about my operation?/Let me tell you about my labor with my first child.

If you take a conversation hostage with this sort of comment, your listener may just give up, waiting for you to talk yourself dry. The conversation won't lead anywhere new for you, and he won't be motivated to pursue acquaintance with you because you aren't interested in him. He will also feel silenced if you follow every story of his with:

> ➤ I can top that . . . ; I can do better than that . . .

> ➤ Well, wait until you hear this!

> ➤ You think that's bad . . .

The "it had to be you" openers are nearly as offensive to most people as those that imply "it had to be me." These lines include inappropriate, nosy questions about another person's health or body:

> ➤ What's wrong with your face?

> ➤ Are you on a diet?/Have you put on weight?

> ➤ I didn't know you were expecting!

> ➤ Are you okay? You look tired.

Also, avoid boorish remarks like:

> ➤ Yuck! How can you eat that?!

- Why don't you have any children?/Why don't you have more children?/Why did you have so many children?
- Why isn't your husband here?
- Who is looking after the baby?

If you choose your opening lines carefully and avoid remarks that are true conversation killers, you can probably find something in common with just about everyone you meet—and have fun doing it. Once you've made your initial connection and navigated the safe terrain of small talk, you can move into the sweet spot of social life—the heart of the conversation.

The Heart of the Conversation

The German philosopher Arthur Schopenhauer grew so tired of the stale conversations of soldiers at his favorite inn that he started a little wager to entertain himself. When he sat down for dinner, he would take out a gold coin and set it on the table. If the soldiers nearby talked about anything but horses, dogs, or women, he would give the coin to the poor at the end of the meal. Most of the time, he would simply put the coin back in his pocket.

Although horses, dogs, and women may not be inevitable topics in the twenty-first century, everyone occasionally gets trapped in predictable ruts that make talk seem trite. Let's explore some ways to keep dynamic conversations going, as well as ways to steer and rescue floundering exchanges.

Follow the Four Steps in Order

Sometimes people get into trouble in conversation because they suddenly express how they feel about something before they have really established any meaningful connection with another person. Europeans, in particular, take offense at Americans who tend to do this.

To avoid the awkwardness that arises from having to backtrack (or backpedal) to a more formal footing, follow the logical progression of a conversation:

STEP 1   Initial courtesies: opening lines and small talk ("I'm Kerry. Haven't I seen you in the Sears Tower elevator?")

STEP 2   An exchange of facts ("Yes, I work for the shoe business on the eighteenth floor.")

STEP 3   Opinions about those facts ("You must have a great view of the new building going up across the street.")

STEP 4   Feelings about the facts ("Actually, I'm really steamed that I won't be able to see the lake anymore.")

If you proceed right to step 3 without gleaning any information ahead of time about the facts at hand (and often before sufficient initial courtesies have been exchanged), you'll sound preachy and close-minded. If you pronounce judgment on something without offering the listener anything more useful than a one-word adjective like "shocking" or "amazing" to describe your feelings, you'll sound shallow and overwrought.

In the same vein, if you rush right into a display of your feelings without bothering to build the framework of a relationship in the first three steps, why should anyone care?

The People You Meet: The Empty Phraser

The empty phraser expresses opinions without paying much attention to the facts. He sees the world in black and white as it relates to himself, and you're either with him or against him. Everything he disapproves of is "crap." He is a master of saying intensifying words over and over again. They fill the air with buzz but have no real substance:

- The play was "astounding."
- The painting was "beautiful."
- The musician was "incredible."
- The restaurant was "fabulous."
- She is reading a "fascinating" book.
- Your dessert was "stunning."
- Her daughter's school is "top-ranked."

The worst offenders use the same phrase to describe everything they talk about. When such a person is finished talking, you don't know anything more than when you started. To engage an empty phraser, try to get him to slow down and tell you what he actually saw or heard. Ask him which songs the musician played, what other books the author has written, or what material the dress was made of—at least you'll go home with a few real details.

The People You Meet: The Instant Old Friend

The instant old friend bypasses the nourishing background of who you are, where you are coming from, or what you are thinking, and goes straight for the sugar rush of dessert—she just wants to tell you her feelings and merge them with yours:

- "I know how you feel because . . ."
- "I felt the same way."
- "I did too."
- And sometimes even "You shouldn't feel that way."

The normal growth of acquaintance usually moves from conventional phrases to sharing of facts, to airing of opinions, to revelation of feelings. The instant old friend takes the two of you immediately to the feeling phase, without establishing any of the intervening structure. Once you have skipped through the normal progression of acquaintance directly to the deepest phase—telling your feelings—you may find that you can't back up and actually find out anything about each other's facts or opinions without a great deal of awkwardness. And there the acquaintance stays—a building on a flimsy foundation.

Two hundred years ago, a diarist described the instant old friend: "She kissed him prettily at the end of the evening. They felt they knew in one evening all they were ever going to know—conversation too ready, not enough reserve; one seemed to empty the whole well in one dip."

If the express lane to intimacy makes you feel uncomfortable, it's too fast. If you find yourself heading right into a cozy friendship with someone you've just met, put on the brakes. To discourage the other person from sharing too many intimacies, change the subject or wrap up the conversation. Don't let yourself get trapped and sucked into the role of therapist. Likewise, save the discussion of your hopes and dreams for the people who already know you well and care about your feelings. Your new friend may well become a confidant someday, but for now, step back and slowly build a foundation.

Stay on Track

To keep the conversation on course, don't steer it into a dead end. Always leave the other person something to reply to. For example, don't:

> ➤ Drag in your experiences from fourth grade if they really don't apply and if the other person doesn't know you well.

> ➤ Explain how you had the worst day last week.

> ➤ Go on and on about a book that you alone have read.

> ➤ Talk about what the reviewer wrote if everyone else has seen the movie (or read the review themselves)—unless they really want to discuss it.

> ➤ Marvel at coincidences. (I was at the mall and guess who I ran into?)

Consider what the take-home point is. Have you exchanged authentic expressions of who you really are? If the person you talked with were asked "What did you two talk about?" would there be anything left that was interesting enough for him to tell the next person? The conversation will be more meaningful if he can take something away from it—if he learned about your own ideas and experiences, not something you heard, something you feel, or something someone else did.

Listen

A good listener is not only popular everywhere but after a while he knows something.
—Wilson Mizner, screenwriter, 1925

You become a good talker by being a good listener, so:

➤ Listen carefully to what people are *trying* to say.

➤ Don't lose eye contact. Keep your facial expression neutral; don't overreact or sit stony-faced.

➤ Nod once in a while to show you are paying attention.

➤ Even if you see the point, don't interrupt.

Don't be afraid to let silence into your conversations. If your mouth is full when someone asks you a question, just hold up a palm or index finger briefly (close to your face or over your mouth) and break eye contact; they'll get the idea to hit the pause button and then resume. You can smile and sit side by side in silence over a meal. (In fact, in many societies people eat in silence as a sign of respect and focus.) If you've both been talking intensely, you can occasionally turn to what is going on around you (other people's activities, music, the room, the food) in companionable semi-silence while your thoughts catch up.

If you get stuck in silence because you don't know what to say, it's not the end of the world. Calvin Coolidge said, "I learned early in life that you never have to apologize for something you didn't say." Have the wisdom to let the other person break the silence.

Speak with Care

Although it's sometimes necessary to ask questions in order to find some common ground with another person, use care to ensure that you are asking appropriate questions.

Quash your assumptions. Don't ask a total stranger who has adopted a child from another country whether she has a fertility problem. Don't make assumptions about a person's background based on his or her accent or skin color. A friend of mine was on a boat cruise around Boston Harbor one summer day when a complete stranger approached him and asked where he was from. (My friend's grandparents came from Armenia, and he has dark skin and eyes.) He told the stranger that he was from Milford, a small town west of Boston. The stranger persisted, "But where are you from originally?" When my friend replied that he was born in this country, the stranger continued, "But how long have you lived here?" The subtext was "You can't be a real American unless your skin is white."

Also, step carefully around the elephant in the room. It's sometimes tricky to navigate a sensitive topic like alcoholism or an annoying distraction that is hard to miss—like the host's dog that is hanging on your leg or the sounds of loud romance coming from the hotel room next door. When in doubt about whether to acknowledge such "elephants" with your words, remember these three tactics: Laugh it off or ignore it (the telltale embarrassing sound); push it off (the dog pawing your knee); and leave the conversational door open (for the friend who is living with an alcoholic). People who are in real trouble will appreciate an opening that allows them to bring up a touchy subject only if they want to.

Watch your words. Speaking with care also means slowing

down and thinking about what you mean to say before something inappropriate comes out of your mouth. Don't go down the following roads:

No puff pieces, trophy talk, or navel news:

➤ Don't brag about your own or your family's achievements. Ditto your good luck and your cleverness.

➤ Don't boast about the virtues of your own generation or condemn the faults of the younger generation, especially in contrast with your own.

➤ Don't fixate on a proprietary pleasure, such as a private club or hobby that your listener doesn't belong to or share.

➤ Do your navel gazing in the privacy of your own home. The details of your interior life are most likely only interesting to a paid therapist.

Skip the verbal padding:

➤ As I said to my wife yesterday . . . (and she probably said "yes dear" with the same weary lack of interest that your listener is feeling right now)

➤ Then I said . . . and she said . . . and I said . . . and she said. . . .

➤ And I'm like . . . and he's like . . . and I'm like . . . and he's like. . . .

➤ I said to myself, I said. . . .

➤ Then I go . . . and then he goes. . . .

➤ And my little cousin got into her little car and drove to her little house ("little" used to demean and belittle)

- At this point in time
- Frankly
- Basically
- Y'know?

Turn off your technobabble:

- Jargon, shoptalk
- Hardware, software, anything known by a number
- A new gadget, especially computer hardware

Saying Good-bye

If you've nothing more to say, then pray, scat!
—From the film *Gentlemen Prefer Blondes,* 1953

All good things—and all good conversations—must come to an end. The purpose of most gatherings is to allow several people to meet one another. Whether you or the person you are talking with indicates that it's time to move on to the next person, don't feel that the conversation has failed or that either one of you is being "blown off." The more graciously you learn to move on, the better. You're both there to circulate.

At MIT's "Magnetic Manager Program," nicknamed the "Charm School," a graduate student asked about the challenge of ending a conversation with one person and moving on to talk with someone else. Kenneth Morse, the founder of the program, suggested, "The most gracious thing to do is say 'I'd like you to meet some of my friends.' Then introduce them and make your graceful getaway." In other words, always end a conversation before it's over.

Get Rid of Verbal Tics

In large measure, polishing your conversational style means getting rid of "verbal tics," those words or phrases that you repeatedly interject but that don't add any meaning to what you are saying. They can be annoying and even distracting depending on how often you utter them.

1. Check yourself for the most common tics: "like, um, you know, er. . . ." Or the newly popular "actually."

2. Know when you're ticking. Leave a tape recorder on the table when you are having an everyday conversation at home or on the phone. Later, listen to the tape, and your tics will jump right out at you.

3. Pay close attention to your speech over the next week and check yourself each time you include your tic words. Maybe pinch yourself each time. Record yourself again a week later to check your progress.

4. Fix your tics with immediate feedback. Ask your loved one to call your attention to your "you knows" with a kick under the table for every ten tics—but don't ask him or her unless you really want to hear the answer and fix it.

5. Allow silence into your sentences. If you can think about what you are going to say ahead of time and slow your speech down, you can begin to banish those useless sounds.

To wrap up a conversation, start winding it down with your body language. Change your posture and break eye contact for a few seconds, then clear your throat, look at your watch, or change your tone of voice. Use kind phrases: "It has been nice talking with you." "It's good to catch up." "I have to go now." "I'm so glad we met." Shake hands, hug, or air-kiss. Say "I really have to go now" and give your head a regretful little shake if the other person keeps talking. *Don't* start a new subject.

You can end most conversations simply with an all-purpose sign-off like "It's been good to see you" or "It was nice meeting you." Here are some other exit lines:

Nature Calls

➤ I need to stretch my legs.

➤ I'm having trouble hearing in this crowd.

➤ Let's go and get more food [or drink].

➤ I have to excuse myself for a moment.

Duty Calls

➤ I have to go help with [something]; I'm going to help in the kitchen.

➤ I need to look after some of my other guests.

➤ I have to talk to someone else here for a while; I need to meet someone here.

➤ I promised my daughter I'd be home by ten.

We Should Mingle

➤ May I introduce you to [innocent bystander].

➤ Let's go around and meet some people.

➤ I'm going to circulate around the crowd.

➤ I don't know anyone here. Can you introduce me to anybody? (Or, if he or she doesn't know anyone either,

"Let's introduce ourselves to some new people.")

Let's Save It for Later

➤ That must have been so hard [interesting, exciting, challenging] for you. I'd love to hear about it when we have another chance to talk.

➤ Do you have a card? I'd like to get in touch with you another time.

Gracious Escapes

➤ It has been interesting talking to you.

➤ I mustn't take up any more of your time.

➤ I'm going to stop before I start to bore you.

This Is Good-bye

➤ See you later. Thanks for telling me about [specifics].

➤ I'll let you go now./I have to go now.

When you leave, say "good night," "good-bye," or "see you soon." Respect others' conventions, and use comic or cozy farewells only if you're sure of your listener. These include:

➤ Bye; Bye-bye; Ciao.

➤ Give my best to your family. Remember me to your wife.

➤ God bless.

➤ Hasta la vista, baby.

Don't end with insincere platitudes. Don't say "We must get together sometime," "Let's do lunch," or "I'll have my people call your people . . ." unless you mean it. "Have a nice day," "Be good," and "Take care" are also pretty overworked. "Be good," "Have fun," or "Drive carefully" are strangely meaningless unless you think about their implications; then they're even stranger. "Have a great day" piles layers of exaggeration, bossiness, and staleness on top of one another.

If you've successfully traveled from hello to good-bye in a conversation with another person, your connection, for now, is complete. When it's time to end that connection, choose your words as carefully as you chose your opening lines. Finish your conversation on a civilized note.

· II ·

Ten Rules of Conversation

What you do not want done to yourself, do not do to others.
—Confucius, *The Confucian Analects*, c. 500 BC

IVILIZED CONVERSATION follows a basic format: greet, talk, and finish. Each conversation will also be shaped by where and who you are, the occasion, and how long you talk. You can, of course, do just what the occasion requires, but every conversation offers you the chance to do more than this minimum. You can be creative in even the most ordinary encounter. In art, the content can always transcend the limits of its container.

Though conversation can follow many paths, there are limits to free expression. If you talk on and on, interrupt someone in mid-sentence, and spread rumors, you'll soon find that you are standing alone with your soliloquy. This chapter covers the basic boundaries of safe speech, starting with the all-important oath: Tell the truth, the whole truth, and nothing but the truth.

Rule 1. Tell the Truth

Truth is always exciting. Speak it, then. Life is dull without it.

—Pearl Buck, *To My Daughters, with Love,* 1967

Conversation must first be truthful. Without honesty, your conversation will be empty. To be honest when you speak, be forthright about who you are; accept the boundaries of truth that you and the other person have agreed on; and share the truth that is palatable and kind—not painful to hear.

No Fooling

Sam: So how's your life?
Karen: Oh, great. How's yours?
Sam: Not so great.
Karen: Ohhh, we're telling the truth.

—From the film *The Big Chill,* 1983

To speak the truth about who you are, be wholly honest and clear about your background, your experiences, and your accomplishments. Don't make the truth larger or smaller than life. Aim for a middle ground between self-praise and false modesty.

A good friend of mine has every right to be proud of a life full of achievement, but in conversation she has to pump everything up even a little more. She sounds like she's a product she's trying to sell, pointing out all the wonderful features that people ought to notice. She describes every vacation as longer than it really was, every unpleasant job as contemptible, every friend as famous, and every school her children attended as high-ranked. After a while, I just want her to let some of the air out of those overinflated tires so they don't give us all such a bumpy ride!

Another friend's career is much more illustrious than he will ever let on. Although he is a respected chemical engineer, when he introduces himself in academic circles, he says, "I'm just a plumber." Although he means to be modest, others sometimes perceive his words as a misleading masquerade—maybe even a camouflaged poke at the enormous egos around him. People sense some complex humor in what he's saying, and sometimes they don't get it.

Don't misrepresent yourself like these friends do. Don't exaggerate by puffing up every bit of information about yourself to impress people, and don't poor-mouth your own abilities. If you do, other people will suspect everything you say. Even worse, you will not be clear.

Tell the whole truth. If you drop the phrase "when I lived in France" into your conversation, don't forget to mention that you lived there only two weeks. If your mother introduces you as her "Harvard-educated" daughter, be sure to eventually mention the fact that you didn't actually stay past sophomore year. If you talk about your insider knowledge from your job in the Capitol, don't forget to add that your job lasted one year—three decades ago.

While you're at it, remember to tell nothing *but* the truth. Don't add, embroider, or expand. If you elaborate and tell more than you need to, people will eventually start to wonder why.

If you tend to exude a sense of inferior self-worth, make an effort to project some confidence into your speech. Whenever you're tempted to demote yourself in conversation, remember the wisdom of Dr. Seuss: "Be who you are and say what you feel, because those who mind don't matter and those who matter don't mind."

The Kindness of Half-Truths

A little sincerity is a dangerous thing, and a great deal of it is absolutely fatal.

—Oscar Wilde, "The Critic as Artist," 1891

Sometimes you need to recognize when being bold-faced is not going to benefit anyone; in fact, the most civilized approach sometimes calls for shading the truth a little—even telling a little white lie. Blunt honesty coexists in a yin-yang relationship with tactful fibbing. Real life doesn't actually offer you many chances to be the heroic little boy who was the only one to say out loud "The emperor has no clothes." More often, the emperor is someone you know, with fragile feelings, whose clothes are just a little tight . . . and you'd never tell him *that*. You can tell when a social fib is called for if the alternative would be hurtful.

The following questions can trip you up, especially if you answer them too quickly without first thinking through the effect that the truth might have on the person who asked:

> *Does this make me look fat?*

  Never say "yes," "not really," "only from the back," or the obvious answer: "I refuse to answer because I don't want you to beat me up." Instead, dissemble a little: "That shirt doesn't flatter you as well as the blue one does. I like the blue one better."

> *Do you like my new haircut?*

  No-win. You could try to get away with "I liked the old one till I saw this new one" or "It suits you."

➤ *Notice anything new?*

Say no and you sound uncaring; say yes and you'll have to identify it, and there's no fun in the game. You might hedge with "Something's different," or "Something different about you. What is it?" but you can't imply that the old version called for a makeover.

➤ *Which dress should I wear tonight?*

Get her to tell you the reasoning behind several choices and let her talk herself into one. Then agree.

➤ *What did you think of my violin solo?*

If you really don't like an artist's work, you don't have to lie, but find something other than a professional yardstick to measure it by. Praise the effort that made it happen, the sincerity that it shows, the artist's progress, and the heart that went into it. Ask him to tell you what it means to him.

➤ *Do you like the present that I gave you?*

Always acknowledge the thoughtfulness of a person's gift, even if it's something that you'll never use. "Thank you so much for thinking of me" is always a safe reply.

For all of these "trick questions," you can respond to the underlying concern rather than the one that has been stated. What she really wants to know is "Do I look okay?" or "Am I still attractive to you?" or "Has my gesture or gift pleased you?" Answer *those* questions. "You look great." "I think you're lovely." "Your gift made me happy—you put so much thought into it." And remember not to ask these questions yourself at the risk of putting other people in an awkward spot.

Truth Before Consequences

For truth itself does not have the privilege to be employed at any time and in every way; its use, noble as it is, has its circumscriptions and limits.

—Michel de Montaigne, *Les Essais,* 1580

While some white lies protect the feelings of the other person, others are purely self-protective. If someone wants you to agree with something shady or unethical or illegal, you don't have "go along to get along" as the old saying goes. Your friend may ask you to say she slept over at your house although she was actually with her boyfriend. A coworker may want you to provide a letter of recommendation for someone you hardly know. Your best friend's brother may want to use your receipt to pad his expenses. Your boss may ask you to sign a loyalty oath you don't believe in. In these instances, use whatever version of the truth will keep your conscience clear. The mild deception of your little white lie will be eclipsed by the other person's big, blinding dishonesty: "I have plans that night"; "I'm too swamped with work to write a thoughtful letter of recommendation"; "My accountant needs all of my receipts"; "I'm not going to do that just now."

Develop some objection-proof defenses, such as "I would not be comfortable doing that," "That would keep me awake at night," "I'm not a good fibber," or "You don't want to ask me to do that; I would confess the truth immediately." If the other person persists, just say a simple no.

The People You Meet: The Shrinking Violet

Sometimes people have a hard time speaking up in any social situation out of shyness. They may feel that they are not worth talking to. Unfortunately, a shrinking violet may be misinterpreted as being aloof when she is simply at a loss for words.

Many introverted people suffer from a kind of sensory overload: they notice too much about their surroundings and their own feelings and they get overwhelmed.

To cultivate the shrinking violet, first identify whether he is actually shy. Then think about what may be making him especially uncomfortable and trim your conversation to help him:

- *Identify the shy person.* Don't be fooled by disguises: many shy people masquerade as curmudgeons, snobs, or blusterers. Not every wallflower is shy, and not every party animal feels confident. A reserved or dignified person is not necessarily shy. The truly shy person is wary; she copes by disengaging.

- *Consider the setting.* Some people aren't comfortable talking in an elevator, chatting with a stranger, or working the room at a party. They may be threatened by noisy crowds, formal occasions, or brief meet-and-greet events.

- *Try to help.* Make eye contact with her, smile, and initiate a conversation. If she seems overwhelmed by the size of the gathering, guide her toward a smaller group or talk with her one on one.

- *Stop talking.* Find a shared nonverbal activity like watching the crowd or listening to music together.

- *Don't use the* s *word.* You can talk about sharing the symptoms of shyness, such as "I don't know anyone here, do you?" or "That's a pretty intimidating lineup of bigwigs." Never say "Don't be shy." Especially to a child.

Rule 2. Don't Ramble

Spare thy flood of talk.
—Aeschylus, *Seven Against Thebes,* 467 BC

Whether your conversational style is one of exquisite refinement or effusive gusto, it's always wise to keep your words short and simple. "I'm sorry to be late. Traffic was terrible" is enough. Don't start to elaborate: "There was this jackknifed tractor trailer on the interstate and we had to sit, and then there were no parking places left and I locked my keys in the trunk." If you continue to ramble on and if you keep piling on excuses, you will sound defensive and your listeners may suspect that you're making the whole thing up.

Rule 3. Don't Interrupt

There are two faults in conversation which appear very different, yet arise from the same root, and are equally blameable; I mean an impatience to interrupt others; and the uneasiness of being interrupted ourselves.
—Jonathan Swift, *Gulliver's Travels and Other Works,* 1726

Just as rambling can keep the spotlight of the conversation on you and your excuses, interrupting can derail a conversation because one person keeps popping up into the spotlight. Either way, interrupting keeps both people from enjoying a balanced exchange.

Job Interview Small Talk

The point of a job interview is for the interviewer to identify your potential, not for you to make friends with her. Nevertheless, the rules of conversation apply:

- Chat about the traffic and weather that you encountered on the way. If possible, make your words reflect the kind of problem solver you are (e.g., "It was snowing hard, but I put on galoshes and walked the ten blocks").

- A good interviewer will make the meeting feel personal enough for his purposes. Don't make the conversation even more chummy by adding useless and potentially negative information.

- Give just the facts about yourself and add a few of your opinions. Don't talk at all about your feelings.

- Your interviewer may be a human resources person whom you may not see again, a staffer who will be a colleague at the same level, or a potential boss. Consider the fact that your conversation during the interview may be the start of a long working relationship.

- When the formal interview comes to an end, it's still not over. As you're winding it up and walking out, don't start to chatter out of pure relief. A brief "Thank you for seeing me" or "I hope to hear from you soon" is sufficient.

Interrupting is the verbal equivalent of shoving. But while most people learn not to shove except in an extreme emergency, interrupters start from birth with the cry in the middle of the night and never move on. As toddlers they like getting what they want when they want it ("Mommy!" "Cookie!"), and they sail into adulthood with their ears closed and their mouths working.

Not all interrupters have bad intentions. Some people interrupt only to agree with what the other person is saying. Other interrupters are shy people who are uncomfortable with silence, so they continually toss in "uh-huhs" to show involvement. Unfortunately, the smartest people are often the worst interrupters because they anticipate where the conversation is going. They get the point, so why wait?

In addition to the fact that interrupting is rude, this habit can land you in conversational quicksand. As the advice columnist Ann Landers said, "The trouble with talking too fast is you may say something you haven't thought of yet."

To prevent yourself from interrupting, slow down. Wait until the other person is completely finished with his sentence and there is a pause for you to begin yours. Don't be afraid of silence. Don't jump into every lull in the conversation. When you're talking with more than one person, rather than jump in with your opinion, turn to the person next to you and hand the conversation off by asking "What do you think?" or "Has this happened to you?"

If, in spite of your best efforts, you do interrupt someone, say, "Excuse me for interrupting. Please continue."

○ ○ ○

The People You Meet: The Schoolmarm

A schoolmarm is a type of thick-skinned extrovert who can wreak havoc with other people's self-esteem. She may have been a teacher at some point in her life. She certainly will correct your grammar if you make a mistake and all but pat you on the head when she approves of what you say. Without meaning to, she can sound patronizing with her tone of voice simply by using the following typical phrases:

- I always say . . .
- Everyone knows. You must know that.
- You can't believe that.
- Let me set you straight on that. Let me tell you about that.
- Actually, it's not.
- I think what you really mean to say is . . .
- You've got that wrong.

These phrases take you right back to the classroom. To engage a schoolmarm, remember that school is out and you are both grown-ups now. Don't let her bossiness or her desire to control your opinion awaken your inner two-year-old.

Steer the conversation with a schoolmarm onto an equal footing by asking factual questions about herself and her life rather than her already settled ideas. Don't challenge her directly or clash with her authority; you might get your knuckles rapped. Step outside her classroom by finding areas where you both have expertise and by including more people in the conversation.

Rule 4. Ask Questions and Listen to the Answers

Harry Burns: You were going to be a gymnast.
Sally Albright: A journalist.
Harry Burns: Right, that's what I said.
—From the film *When Harry Met Sally,* 1989

No one likes to be interrupted, but everyone likes to be heard. Being considerate in conversation thus means that you show the other person that you're interested in what he has to say and you're willing to really tune into his words.

Begin with a Question

When you're getting acquainted with someone, a good way to launch a dialog is to say the person's name and begin with a genuine question. For instance, "John, did you go to Brown as a graduate student?" Or "Do you find it hard to switch back and forth between English and Farsi, Yanina?"

"Most people are more interested in their business and life than yours," advises MIT's Kenneth Morse, "so draw them out." Five students from MIT's Sloan School of Management attended a networking event to meet job recruiters. Ahead of time, their course instructors told the students to find out enough about the recruiters to know what would interest them. Each time the students met a recruiter, they only asked questions. The next day, Morse asked the recruiters about the event. They said that they were impressed with the Sloan students and wanted to hire them.

The questions you ask shape the conversation you get. Make them essay questions, such as "What did you do on Christmas?" rather than yes-or-no questions like "Have you taken down the

Five Fail-Safe Starters

Your follow-up to "nice to meet you" or "good to see you again" is the test of your conversational finesse. Here are a few tried and true starting points:

- *The journey.* Ask "How did you get here?" with a time frame ranging from a few hours to a few years to a lifetime. "Did you come on foot or in a car?" "How did you decide to move here from Detroit?" "Are you from here or did you move here? When? Why?"

- *The recent past.* "What have you been working on lately?" "How is business these days?" or "Are you just back from (or off to) somewhere interesting?"

- *The situation you share now.* "How do you know the host?" "Do you know when the subway will be running again?" "What did you think of that speech?"

- *Companions.* "Do you have family nearby?" or "Is your family from the area?" Not everyone has children or a spouse; virtually everyone has family.

- *The return question.* "But what about *your* work (or *your* family, travel, hobby)?" People almost always want you to ask them what they just asked you.

tree yet?" Then listen to the response. Pace yourself with one question at a time. Don't interrogate people.

Listen to the Answer

When you ask an opening question, skip the pro forma inquiries, especially if you're not really interested in the answers.

Don't ask how a person's children are doing if you don't really know them. In fact, never ask about anything unless you're prepared to listen to the answer. Don't toss off a "throwaway" question, like a bone that you'd give a puppy to gnaw on, while you glance around the room in search of someone else who is more interesting.

After you ask a question, be an intelligent, involved listener, not just a listening post. Pay the person the compliment of responding, asking more, talking about your side of the topic, and occasionally rephrasing what she said to show that you are buying in to some of it. If the other person answers that she enjoyed a recent exhibit, for instance, ask which painting or piece of sculpture in particular appealed to her. If he watched the Super Bowl, ask if he played football in high school.

This rule applies to conversations with new acquaintances as well as to conversations with people you know well. As the sociologist Robert Lynd said, "A man may forgive many wrongs, but he cannot easily forgive anyone who makes it plain that his conversation is tedious."

Hit the Ball Back

Once you've asked a question and the other person has replied, don't just agree and soothe and mirror and conciliate; send the ball back across the net when he volleys. An attitude of "Now that's interesting, I've always wanted someone to explain it to me" is much more provocative than "Oh, really?" Being an active listener has benefits for both of you. Don't just absorb ideas; send some ideas back.

The People You Meet: The Interviewer

The interviewer will emit a string of noncommittal, encouraging responses that keep you talking about your topic without revealing anything about herself. Lawyers do this when they take a deposition, journalists when they interview a subject, psychologists when they evaluate a person's problem. You will go home all talked out, but none the wiser about the person you just talked to.

At a fundraising dinner, my friend Candace was thrilled to find herself seated next to a famous radio interviewer. They talked a blue streak about book illustration and eighteenth-century music. She was a little shy about talking so much, but he seemed so impressed with her ideas and knowledge that she held forth a bit on her specialty.

Only a few days later did it dawn on her that he was just doing that evening what he did all day: he was encouraging her to talk, making her feel fascinating, helping her put her thoughts into the most eloquent words. Nothing wrong with that, but she had not learned anything about him except what he had reflected back to her about herself. She'd had a great, head-spinning experience, but she couldn't even begin to assess whether she had reciprocated. She had been in the hands of a master interviewer.

If your listener is using phrases like "Tell me more," "That's fascinating," "Really?" and "How did you feel about that?" wake up and reciprocate. You can draw these neutral, agreeable people out by asking for their opinions and inquiring about their interests, hobbies, travels, and enthusiasms. Answer their questions; then ask them the same questions: "And how do *you* feel about that?"

Watch for clues to what is behind the mask. Do some homework to find out what they are really interested in.

Rule 5. Don't Take Advantage of People

Conversation is most civilized when it is founded on equality. It's unequal if one of you gets more out of the conversation, or if one of you has a practical use for the other. Conversation at its best is not a zero-sum transaction, where you get more only if the other person gets less; rather, it is a creative process where you each take home more than you brought.

Be Balanced

If you are unhappy and the attention is all on you, the other person has given up some attention that she may need. Also, when you are happy and keep the focus of the conversation on yourself, your well-wishers may feel happy for you, but you haven't generated much for them. When a friend with a column in the local newspaper grabs you at a concert to find out what is going on at city hall, you may help her know more, but you won't be any better informed in return. When you gush about your crush to a friend, or even to the one you adore, you leave no room for the person to say anything that gets through the mist of your emotions.

If you are asking for sympathy in some private misery, and the other person has really heard you out, let him know how much you appreciate it and how much it has helped: "I feel so much better when I talk with you. You help me to remember that I'm not the only person to go through a difficult divorce."

While you soak up the spotlight as the happy couple or guest of honor, remember to reflect some light back onto your guests: "This means so much more because you are celebrating with us."

The Doctor Is Out

Tempting as it may be, meeting a professional of any sort—doctor, lawyer, teacher, state trooper—at a party is not an invitation to milk him or her about what might be causing your headaches or how much it costs to sue an ex-husband. Expert advice from professionals is valuable; it's linked to years of training. By using it as a party trick, you trivialize both the advice and the person and ask, in effect, for the person to help you cheat him or her out of an office fee. Some people in the "helping professions" are especially prone to being targeted for free advice. You wouldn't ask a clothing designer for a free blouse or a contractor to step into your kitchen and sand your floor for free during a party. Don't ask other professionals for free "goods" either.

When you meet such a person, after you have talked about mutually interesting topics, sound him out about talking shop before you launch into an off-site office visit. Say "Do you object to hearing about people's knees when you're off duty? I've got to find a specialist for my mother," rather than "Gee, maybe you could tell me what to do about this pain I get every time I do this," or "Knees, huh? Well, I heard about a guy whose doctor operated on the wrong knee." A doctor friend of mine turns off the most boorish talkers' requests with a humorous reply: "We can have a look at your problem right now if you'll just start by taking off all your clothes."

In a social setting, don't look for sympathy or try to short-circuit the need for a real consultation. But do keep asking questions if you are genuinely interested in what the person does. Find out about who she is, not what she can do for you. Ask "Has perfume designing changed much in the last ten years?" and "Tell me how job sharing works for you" and "How did you choose your specialty?"

If a professional *is* willing to talk with you about his work, instead of asking for free advice, ask what he would advise you to do next or whom to see: "If you were looking for a surgeon to operate on your mother, whom would you choose?"

Don't ever draft a person unwittingly into your conversational army. Always consider the fact that he may have agreed with you simply to be agreeable in the setting that you shared. For instance, if he is a lawyer who will talk with you about your divorce, don't use his seeming approval of your idea about custody as a free endorsement when you sit down with your own attorney. No matter what kind of expertise she has, don't ever invoke her opinion for leverage later on in an argument, as in "Katy thinks it would be a good idea if . . ." or "Page agrees with me that we should . . ." or "I asked Laura and she thought that would be wonderful. What do you think?"

Pro Bono Boundaries

Once in a while, all friends turn to each other for volunteer expertise, free therapy, and unpaid advice. When you are the one who needs assistance, be clear with the other person that you'd like to try a different format from your usual conversations. She probably won't feel taken advantage of if you describe what you need and acknowledge that you're requesting a special, temporary conversational style, not a new norm in your friendship.

Then you and your friend can simply agree about what you need from her: to be a sounding board that gives your ideas a reality check; to provide a shoulder to cry on; to advise you on a topic in which she has expertise; to do peer counseling in which you each listen to the other for half an hour at a time without interrupting; or to play devil's advocate by finding the weak spots in your reasoning.

Be clear about the limited duration of this setup and your willingness to turn the tables and play the role of free therapist when need be. That way, this kind of conversation can feel more like a generous barter and less like being mugged.

Rule 6. Don't Dwell on Appearances

Taking advantage of another person is in bad form because it turns a talk into a transaction. Likewise, dwelling on personal appearance is seldom a safe or an uplifting topic for civilized conversation because it takes the focus off the whole person and limits the discussion to superficialities. In either case, the conversation is drained of its potential to become something richer and more meaningful.

You must not greet a tall person with "How's the weather up there?" or accuse him of making you feel short. Similarly, don't comment on the weight of a fat person, regardless of whether he has lost weight or gained more. Don't tell a pregnant woman that she is "absolutely enormous." And don't tell a thin person how much you hate and envy her, especially if she has turned down dessert and you've had seconds.

Such tacky comments are toxic to conversations because it's hard to move beyond them. To comment is to take the first step in judging, and judging has big risks and small rewards. Whether you flatter them to their faces or pass judgment behind their backs, when you judge people on how they look, you risk at least a dozen mistakes:

> ➢ To say something is to imply the opposite might even be thinkable. When you say "Mike looked good tonight," you

imply that he sometimes doesn't. "Black is so thinning" suggests that a person would look heavy in a lighter color.

➤ Even positive judgments imply that you are entitled to comment. When you say "I like that hair color," you imply that your approval somehow matters in the other person's decision-making process.

➤ Often the judgment is comparative: someone has to lose for someone else to win. "Your dress is prettier than Caroline's" makes any decent woman feel protective of Caroline and guilty about herself. As Dogberry the watchman says in Shakespeare's *Much Ado about Nothing*, "Comparisons are odorous."

➤ You risk showing that you don't understand a person's motivation. "What's with that hat?" will mark you as a clueless geek if ski caps are fashionable.

➤ You often hurt her feelings, whether you mean to or not: "Is your collar supposed to stick up like that?"

➤ You may overlook what the person would like you to notice. "You're the tallest girl in the chorus" may dishearten a young lady who wants to be noticed for her beautiful voice.

➤ You reveal your own moral failings. If your first comment about a common acquaintance is "She's not very pretty, is she?" it shows that you don't value a person's heart, soul, or mind as much as her face.

➤ You reveal your own weakness and leave yourself open to being judged by your own standards. The fellow who mutters "What a dog!" about a woman is often a homely guy projecting his own insecurity.

{ 63 }

➤ Comments about a person's looks often stop the conversation in its tracks. How can she reply to a comment like "You're so gorgeous" or a backhanded compliment like "You wear the most outrageous outfits"?

➤ You may focus on something that the other person doesn't like to have noticed. "Your face-lift looks good" can be a friendship-killer if you say it in a crowd—and she hasn't discussed it with anyone but you.

➤ You risk damning with faint praise when you pay a lukewarm compliment like "She has such a pretty face" (about a fat girl).

➤ Your own apparent motives may offend others. Attractive girls are usually tired of hearing "You're beautiful." People who say that usually want a shortcut to friendship or romance. Their comments practically shout "I don't actually care what you're like inside; the outside is good enough for what I want."

If you absolutely must comment on appearance, don't make a big deal out of it. Reassure a little girl with "You look just right" or "I'm sure people will like what you have on." And whenever possible, stick to "just the facts, ma'am." Admire the color, the cut (without getting into designer labels), or an accessory note. You might even try, with someone you think will tolerate it, that sincerest form of flattery: "Where did you get it?"

Look at the whole person. Don't automatically make a stale comment on what you see; think about what is happening from the other person's point of view. A pregnant woman doesn't need to hear "You're bigger" or "How's the fat lady?" when you could choose from so many engaging topics, such as how excited she is about the future, what the baby's room will look like, where she is planning to give birth, what's on her short list of names, and how she keeps looking so nice when her feet have grown two sizes. When your neighbor's child comes charging in from an hour of play in the rain, don't blurt out "You're really dirty," "What a mess you are!" or "Look at the mud on your clothes!" Instead, say "You look like you've had a great time" or "Let me get you a towel while you tell me about the game."

Don't tell an eighty-year-old woman "You look good for some-one your age" or "You must have been a beautiful woman" unless you want her to think "You must have been a cute baby before you could talk." Instead, ask her about things that maturity makes her good at or that are universal to any age.

Finally, leave your own appearance off the agenda. Vanity is never interesting. Don't fish for compliments by simpering about your own height or thinness. Don't moan about your recent weight gain or blather on about the latest diet. Don't make excuses for trivial flaws in your outfit ("I couldn't find a scarf to accent this coat" or "My socks don't match today" or "I usually don't wear red"). Save the news of any kind of appointment for personal grooming for your own calendar; talk about who you are inside, where it counts, not about the hair coloring, manicures, and Botox treatments that you subject yourself to in order to dress up what's on the outside.

Rule 7. Don't Touch Taboo Topics

Life is livable because we know that wherever we go most of the people we meet will be restrained in their actions towards us by an almost instinctive network of taboos.

—Havelock Ellis, *Selected Essays,* 1936

All cultures have topics that people don't discuss in normal, civilized conversation. Early in life, people learn to avoid these forbidden subjects; it is hard for them to change their attitudes when they are grown. In China, people ask point-blank how much money you earn but stonewall when you ask about their family. In the United States, you can go into detail about your child's toilet training but not about your drinking problem. In Mediterranean Europe and South America, you don't start talking business until you have gotten to know about each other's values, intellect, and families. No matter where you are or how you rationalize it, if you continue to talk about these taboo subjects after people have responded to your initial comments with signals of surprise and dismay, you will offend them.

While hot buttons vary from place to place, in American culture today you will be safe if you steer clear of sex, religion, and politics. It's also wise to withhold unsolicited advice on any topic, especially on how others choose their companions, pick a mate, and discipline their children.

Another special taboo in our culture is related to the dollar sign that may be used to measure a person's social value. Questions about a person's clothes, tuition, house, car, and neighborhood can all smack of assessing his success. If you are asked to put monetary values on things in your life, try to diplomatically avoid it. Get the conversation off possessions and onto events and ideas.

Regardless of where you live, the principle is the same: if you raise topics that people have strong opinions about, you risk ending the discussion in disagreement, possibly derailing the friendship. Taboo topics are connected to ingrained beliefs that a person can't change or is loath to change. People are strongly committed to their opinions on these topics—like brand loyalty. These topics are personal, not logical; the facts differ for each person and thus are not up for argument.

Avoid not just talking about money, but bragging about how much more your vacation house is worth now than when you bought it. Not just feminism, but angry stereotypes about the opposite sex. Not just sex, but other private body matters, such as symptoms of illness and the digestive process.

Taboo topics can disrupt the normal sequence of a healthy, civilized conversation by jumping straight from conventional greetings to opinions and feelings if you don't take the time to first establish and discuss facts. In general, don't start conversations about taboo topics unless you are very well acquainted with the other people in the group already, and be prepared to change the subject when others do. Save these discussions for people you know well.

If you insist on exploring these issues, be aware of the fact that taboo subjects can lead to dangerous conversational waters, even if you presume that others share your point of view. Otherwise, you may find yourself in an argument with no exit. Even people who do agree with your views about personal habits, child rearing, religion, and politics can seem self-righteous and preachy, and you may slide into a pointless dispute. Nobody can win these arguments. Accept the fact that you are not going to cover or solve, with a few minutes' discussion, the question of whether hard or soft discipline is better for children, whether college admissions should be weighted toward minorities, whether the way young people dress is an insult to their elders, whether fundamentalists in any religion are wrong or right, whether FDR was a great president, or whether women with young children ought to work or stay at home to raise their children. It is more important to get to know each other.

Purging your talk of taboos does not mean that your conversation has to be bland. In fact, if you stick only to innocuous chat, you will not learn anything about others or yourself. Differing opinions, voiced by people who have faith in their listener's willingness to consider them, are the backbone of interesting talk and healthy relationships. Sharing opinions is more productive if you go looking for areas where you can learn something from each other—that is, if you avoid the subjects that will never lead you to common ground. A civilized conversation is an art because it can transform people's ideas. If you're not willing to change your own mind about a topic and you know that the person with whom you are speaking won't change his mind either, just don't bring it up.

Rule 8. Disagree in a Civilized Fashion

Just because I disagree with you doesn't mean I'm disagreeable.
—Film producer Sam Goldwyn, 1879–1974

When someone disagrees with you strongly, do you soothingly change the subject? Ask why he seems upset? Contradict? Look for a way to compromise? Act annoyed and shout that he has offended you?

What about when someone offends you on purpose? Do you ask her to retract or clarify the offending comment? Fall into icy silence? Change the subject? Insult her right back? Walk away?

An emerging disagreement can be transformed into either a lively discussion or an unproductive argument. Your tone of voice and the words you choose can sharpen or soften a potential dispute. Body language makes a difference. A friend of mine who is an expert at conflict resolution suggests that when you're face-to-face in a disagreement with someone, don't back up, but move sideways a little. Don't cross your arms or legs. Don't threaten with your physical position or stare and glare at the other person.

Sometimes the best way to disagree is to agree. Sidney Morgan-besser, a legendary professor of philosophy at Columbia University, had to deal with many overblown and ill-informed arguers. He would co-opt the person's position by asking him or her for more detailed information. Just by saying with complete and genuine sincerity, "Now let me see if I understand your thesis . . . ," and by repeating back what he had heard, he would inevitably expose the argument's weak spots.

Everyone can learn to disagree politely, in a friendly, nonconfrontational tone of voice. For instance, if you would genuinely like to hear the other person's opinion and discuss your differences without either caving in or getting overheated, these phrases are useful:

➢ You'd be surprised . . .

➢ There are two sides to that . . .

➢ Let me see if I understand your point of view . . .

➢ Not everyone sees it that way.

➢ I guess we disagree on that.

➢ I understand your point of view. Here's what I think . . .

How to Tell a Joke

Timely, topical, and inoffensive jokes can make ordinary conversations especially fun. But being truly funny requires doing it right!

- If you aren't a natural joke teller or you tend to forget punch lines, practice the whole joke ahead of time. A phrase like "I hope I can remember this . . ." will make your listeners' hearts sink. Don't make them play a question-and-answer game to drag the gag out of you.

- Size up your audience and where the conversation is heading, and signal clearly that you are going to tell a joke. Make sure it relates to the conversation, and keep it brief and direct.

- Choose only fresh and appropriate jokes. If you've told a joke more than twice, probably someone in the group has heard it already. Say "Stop me if you've heard this" and mean it—be prepared to stop. Avoid sexual, racial, or political jokes if you have the slightest doubt about the group's sensitivities.

- Go easy on irony—it's usually not funny. It comes off as sarcasm, and sarcasm comes off as bitterness. A little bit goes a long way.

- Don't short-circuit someone else's joke or immediately try to top theirs with another one. If your joke doesn't fly, just laugh at yourself. If it does fly, stop while you're ahead—it's best, to quote the title of the famous Milton Berle film, to "always leave them laughing."

Some people don't mind these words of disagreement if they are conveyed in the right tone of voice:

Curious and Quizzical

➤ Do you really believe that?

➤ Is that always true?

➤ Are you sure? I heard it differently.

Calm and Rational

➤ I got a somewhat different impression.

➤ I don't agree.

➤ I see your point, but . . .

➤ What is the source of your information?

➤ Is that based on experience or theory?

Bemused

➤ G'wan!

➤ No way!

➤ You don't say!

No tone of voice can make these fighting words belong in civilized conversation:

➤ No, you're wrong. / Nobody believes that! / That's not true.

➤ I don't know what you're smoking, but . . .

➤ Are you kidding? / Are you crazy?

➤ See? I knew you'd say that.

If the person with whom you are speaking really wants to continue, if you can, frame the discussion so that it does not touch on personalities. Reinforce the idea that there are several points of view. Reiterate your own willingness to hear other ideas. If you expect to influence others, be prepared for others to influence you too. The economist John Maynard Keynes said, "When the facts change, I change my mind. What do *you* do?"

If things get acrimonious and people seem to be losing their tempers, try to table the discussion, while you firmly but politely stick to your position. Here are some exit strategies:

> ➤ Let's discuss this some other time.

> ➤ I have to go soon.

> ➤ We'll have to agree to disagree.

> ➤ That's a TWIDY [that's the way I do it] issue. (Especially good when "Because I'm the mom" won't quite do.)

Watch out for people who announce "I love a good argument" or "I'll go to the mat on that issue," as if this exempts them from the laws of civility. Sadists also enjoy the discomfort of others. A dedicated arguer may not pay attention to your ideas or seek common ground, and he will usually ignore your signals that you've reached your limit. He may reply to any mild protests on your part with "You're too sensitive." He may impose the worst aspects of a formal debate onto the weakest areas of argument.

A poor conversationalist may be under the impression that he is entitled to argue because debate is a good thing. A good debater, however, is skilled in arguing either side of an issue, irrespective of his own beliefs. Such a person enjoys the challenge regardless of his own feelings on the topic. In real debates, also, a moderator ensures that both sides get equal time. But that's a good debate, not a good conversation.

○ ○ ○

The People You Meet: The Button Pusher

The test of good manners is to be patient with bad ones.
—Solomon ibn Gabirol, *The Choice of Pearls*, c. 1050

A button pusher looks for the hot buttons in any conversation and continues to push them. A true quarreler, a button pusher is a confronter who puts you on the defensive before you've even said anything. He might say:

- You've changed your hair!
- You know what your problem is?
- You seem to think that . . . /I think what you're trying to say is . . . /I think what you really want is . . .
- I called you but you never pick up!
- You've been back five days and you didn't call?

Don't let this person push your buttons or make you argue back or cave in. Display a kind of neutral, amused detachment and change the subject. I had a lot of trouble not feeling defensive when I talked to Herbert, who used criticism to help him control people and situations. If a phone call was disconnected, he would come back on the line with "You cut me off!" If he ran into an acquaintance, he would start the conversation with "You've been avoiding me." He could make "I haven't seen much of you lately" sound like an accusation of neglect—and get you to feel guilty before you reminded yourself that you had just called him up last week.

In spite of his aggression, he had a good friend, Karl, to whom he seemed devoted. So I watched them carefully one evening to see how Karl made it work. Herbert greeted him with "Where have you been all this time?" and Karl just laughed and answered with a smile, "Crawling here on my hands and knees. I hope you're properly grateful!"

Herbert eyed Karl's dinner and said, "How can you stand that kind of salad? You're not going to eat that garbage, are you?" Karl shot back, in a joking tone, "I only do it to annoy you." I began to grasp that tone of voice made all the difference. While some people may be just too coarse for your own taste, you can appreciate them if you learn to treat their aggressiveness as part of a back-and-forth racquet sport.

Rule 9. Don't Be a Bore

It's all right to hold a conversation, but you should let go of it now and then.

—Richard Armour, columnist, 1906–1989

It is uncivilized to bore people because it means you are not paying attention to them. To prevent yourself from being a bore:

> ➤ Pause for a long breath: Does anyone else speak up?

> ➤ Does anyone ask you a question that encourages you to continue speaking?

> ➤ Do people try to chime in with their own ideas?

- ➤ Have you asked anyone a question lately that would give him or her an opening?

- ➤ Never speak uninterrupted for more than four minutes at a time.

- ➤ If you are the only person who still has a plate full of food, stop talking.

- ➤ Check your audience: Are your listeners really with you? Do they wear a glazed, tuned-out expression? Are they looking away or drifting away? Is your spouse kicking your ankle under the table, rolling his eyeballs, or drawing his forefinger across his throat? Is the waiter hovering to take your order or clear the dishes?

Always consider the possibility that you can bore people—and take precautions. As the statesman Lord Chesterfield said, "Talk often but never long; in that case, if you do not please, at least you are sure not to tire your hearers." You're almost never boring if you talk less than you listen.

Does everybody bore you? If you meet more than the occasional bore, maybe you don't know how to be interested in people. To make sure that you're not the bore in the equation, watch for these signs:

- ➤ People try to interrupt you, but you resist because what you are saying seems so important to you.

- ➤ You often tell the same half-dozen canned anecdotes that feature yourself, whether they really relate to the topic or not.

- ➤ When you tell a story, you give a lot of unnecessary detail.

Conversation Pieces

Conversation pieces are accessories or objects so remarkable that they can inspire conversations and even break the ice with strangers. If you wear one or have one on the table or around your house, have your answer ready, because people will keep commenting on it.

If people are sure to compliment the "gilded macaroni" jewelry that your child gave to you or the six-foot replica of an Egyptian mummy in your living room, think about how to go beyond "thank you" when you respond. Consider several openings that will quickly get the conversation off the object and onto ideas and opinions. "I got it on sale" is not nearly as interesting as "I bid for it at the Greeley Hospital auction" or "I looked all over Greece for a blue tablecloth and finally found the perfect one at the airport. Have you ever done that?" or "I like it too. I got it with the first money I ever earned, as a camp counselor in South Dakota. Can you remember what you did with your first wages?"

If you are the one who is making the compliment about a conversation piece, remember that—as with any form of conversation—context matters. Different cultures have different customs about how to respond to praise. In the United States, such compliments are usually welcome. Compliment a Japanese man and he will say something negative about how unworthy the object is of your notice. Compliment an Indian and he will feel obligated to give it to you as a gift. Compliment an Englishman and he will be mildly offended that you mentioned it at all.

➤ Your listeners often say "I mustn't take up any more of your time" (or other exit lines from chapter I) when they mean *you* mustn't take up any more of *their* time.

Ask the general opening questions that are listed in chapter I—and then be interested in the answers. Learn to keep the conversation moving, like a good game of Frisbee. When you receive it, toss it to someone else within a minute or after a few sentences. And try to dilute your own potential to bore in social gatherings by finding groups of three to five people; then you can just listen while you look intelligent. Remember, people always think you're interesting if you're interested in *them*.

If people seem bored by you, maybe you are not respecting the context of the conversation. For instance, don't take it personally if as a spouse you are not the main attraction at your partner's business gatherings, or if you are a baseball fan in a crowd of book lovers. Just smile and listen. "Restrain your character a little," advised St. José Escrivá; "don't strive to be the salt in every stew." And don't expect to fascinate people at a social event with details of your life at the office. In social or business settings, do some homework to learn people's names, know who might like to talk about what, and brush up your brain in general to make yourself more fun to talk to. Read up on the group in a professional journal or magazine.

"I wish you would read a little poetry sometimes. Your ignorance cramps my conversation," said the novelist Sir Anthony Hope Hopkins. Tap into what you know and consider which interests you might share with others so you have more to offer when you speak or listen.

The People You Meet: The Bore

Then he will talk—good gods! How he will talk!

—Nathaniel Lee, *The Rival Queens; or
The Death of Alexander the Great*, 1677

He talks mainly about himself. He makes you uncomfortable. He is downbeat or overly upbeat about himself. No one else joins your conversation. You feel your world getting smaller. A good conversation makes you feel like you matter, but a bore doesn't even seem to hear what you say. He expresses:

- The same things he said to you the last time you talked with him (and the same things you have overheard him saying to others), often using exactly the same phrases and gestures.

- Long anecdotes about himself.

- Secondhand opinions.

- Stories about the place he's visited and the people he knows as if they were his private property, without ever asking you if you have been there or know them too.

- One-upmanship; he has to top every achievement or difficulty of yours. He's always faster and smarter, or sicker and more injured, or funnier.

- Interest in discussing business in a social setting and vice versa.

All bores are boring because they don't know they are boring or even consider it as a remote possibility. No amount of subtle, courteous signals from you will alert them. The true bore will readily waste your time without gratitude, and you will miss out on conversations you may have preferred. And in the end, after all your endurance, the bore may find *you* boring.

If you're stuck with a bore at a party, remain standing up. At a dinner party, check the place cards and plead with the seating arranger beforehand if possible ("I was hoping to spend the evening with someone new. I know Bob Boring already; can you put me near Frances Fascinating?"). Don't sit down until a few people have arrived. If necessary, issue a disclaimer ("Oh, we see each other all the time"). If this doesn't work, go for damage control—introduce the bore to the people sitting on your other side and help them talk across you.

Always be civilized. Even boring individuals should be treated with courtesy. Give him or her at least five minutes of your time. Don't interrupt, yawn, lose eye contact, or leave without an "excuse me." However, recognize when, in addition to boring you, a bore may drive away the people you want to meet. You have to cut your losses and make a clean getaway. Follow the previous general suggestions for ending a conversation. Chances are the bore is so wrapped up in himself he won't notice your exit.

Rule 10. Don't Gossip

Impart to none what you would not have all know. For some men are moved to tattle by various motives—some through folly, some for gain, some from an empty desire to be thought knowing.
—Francesco Guicciardini, *Counsels and Reflections*, sixteenth century

A well-worn adage is "Dull people talk about things, ordinary people talk about people, fascinating people talk about ideas." If you have graduated from the dullness of talking about things, take care to make your ordinary talk as good as it can get by avoiding gossip when you talk about people. Likewise, steer clear of insider trading and name-dropping.

The tendency to spread information about others is an age-old problem, and to some extent it's probably part of human nature. In fact, the word *gossip* has Old English origins that mean "kinsman," and in early American times, the words *gossip* and *friend* were interchangeable. Today the word connotes sometimes harmful rumors about others. As the philosopher Bertrand Russell said, "No one gossips about other people's secret virtues." If you aren't sure if it is gossip, use the acid test: Would you say it if the person were actually there? If not, it's gossip. Gossip also has a shaky relation to the truth and a murky quality in its origins. It is often third- or fourth-hand, or worse, and it gets less and less accurate with every retelling.

Stop and check for motivation. Is the gossip (we'll assume it's not you) trying to be part of the in group, dominate the conversation, be the first with the news, or scoop some other gossip? Gossips are passive-aggressive, controlling kinds of people. Even positive gossip—about pregnancy or business success—is about control; the gossip appoints herself the information officer, taking that control away from its owner. Gossip is a weapon that makes the powerless feel important. It can be a tool of targeted revenge or simple unfocused ill will. It also isn't civil to use inside information to make another person feel like an outsider. By spreading gossip, you suggest that you are a person in the know and the other person is out of the loop.

You know it's gossip if it divides your loyalty between the group listening and the person being talked about.

Gossip resembles a virus that infects one person after another, with one important difference. While you're usually powerless against a virus, you can decline to "catch" a piece of gossip. You can refrain from passing it on; sometimes you can even refuse to listen to it. Try saying, the next time the gossip bug hits someone near you, "I just don't like to listen to gossip" or "Please, I don't like gossip," and mean it enough to disengage and move away if it continues. People will learn fast not to gossip at or around you.

Also, consider how to keep your own confidential information (about work or family) out of public circulation. As a rule, don't discuss strife between family members, bad bosses, therapy or medical issues, or your child's vulnerabilities. Every time you boast or complain about your teenagers, you risk spreading a form of gossip. If they wouldn't like to hear you say it, don't do it.

Gossip is the subject of a traditional parable. A neighbor overheard the local rabbi discussing a relative's son who was arrested for stealing, and he mistook the name for the rabbi's own son. He breathlessly spread the rumor that the rabbi's son was a thief until the whole town had heard, and the story got back to the rabbi. The rabbi confronted the man, who apologized and asked what he could do to make amends to the boy. The rabbi said, "I can forgive you if you will first take this pillow and slit it open on that nearby hilltop on a windy day." The man did so and returned. The rabbi then said, "Now go and gather up the feathers and put them back in the cover and give them to my son." Then the man understood that no matter how sorry he felt, he could never make up to the rabbi for the damage the rumor did to his son.

Like anyone who grew up in a small town, I know how rapidly and irreversibly gossip can spread and how it feels when the details of your private life circulate in distorted and debased retellings by people who clearly don't bear their subject any goodwill. Almost anything that's told gets retold. I'm also the youngest child, and I learned early on about how unpopular the tattletale can be. Don't play the role of either the first teller or the virus-passer. Remind yourself of the old-fashioned Golden Rules for Conversation posted in elementary school classrooms throughout the twentieth century: "Is it kind? Is it true? Is it necessary?" If what you're saying about someone cannot meet this test, then leave it unsaid.

If you still like to talk about people and don't mind being known to enjoy gossip, try to offer only out-of-date gossip or movie-star gossip.

○ ○ ○

The People You Meet: The Gossip

Yea, as fascinating as a loose tooth is a secret to a young maid.
For she knoweth not whether to spit it out or keep it safe;
yet she cannot forget it.
—Gelett Burgess, *The Maxims of Methuselah,* 1907

One of the most awkward challenges during a conversation can occur when a blabbermouth begins to gossip. Be alert to typical adolescent phrases, such as:

- Don't tell anyone.
- Don't say I told you.
- Your so-called best friend said something about you behind your back.
- I shouldn't tell you this, but . . .
- Did you hear about . . .?/Did you hear what happened to so-and-so?
- Isn't it awful about . . .?

Turn this person off as soon as you can. Without setting yourself up as a prude, use an excuse like "Oh, I'm not a good person to tell a secret to." If he persists, stop him in his tracks with some relentlessly upbeat item about a mutual acquaintance. Try to ignore any tales he tells you about what might be said about you behind your back.

Other responses to stop gossip are:

- You don't want to tell me that.
- I don't need to know that.
- Does [the person] know that you're telling me this?
- Is this private information?
- I'll wait until the facts are in on that.
- I think we can be more charitable.
- Do you think that [person] wants this known and talked about?
- Don't believe every piece of gossip that you hear from that source.
- I don't listen to that sort of thing.

Sometimes you can cut off gossip by calling its newsworthiness into question. Ask: "Do you really want to keep that old rumor going?"

Don't report hurtful comments back to the subject; it seldom helps the injured person. Instead of saying to Amanda that "Jane is telling everybody about your speeding ticket," have the courage to confront Jane yourself and say, "I think you should stop gossiping about Amanda."

Truth forms the touchstone of all rules of conversation, from simply being honest about who you are to thinking carefully before you talk about others. These rules will free you to speak well; they are not designed solely to spoil your fun. If you follow these guidelines, you won't have to learn the hard way how a conversation can fall short of its potential. Trust who you are and what you have to contribute, and your conversation will build connections that are worth having.

· III ·

Rescue Conversations
from Blunders

Discretion in conversation is more important than eloquence.
—Baltasar Gracián, *Oráculo Manual y Arte de Prudencia,* 1647

CIVILIZED CONVERSATION should be warm; it has a life of its own that allows people's ideas to grow. Boredom can freeze the life out of conversation, while argument can burn it up. If you heed the ten rules that I introduced in the last chapter, you will keep your conversation in the temperate zone between frosty and sizzling. Still, between these two extremes you sometimes can make a false step, a faux pas, by saying something careless, unintentional, and genuinely offensive. When you stumble, you must take care not to fall flat on your face, or at least learn to regain your balance quickly. This chapter provides the tools to reorient a conversation that has blundered off the path.

One of my most awkward blunders, which occurred at a festival of early music, was doubly awkward because I had a second chance to avoid it and didn't. My husband's boss introduced me to a local critic who had the last name of (we'll call him) Corelli, "a direct descendant of the composer!" I hoped I didn't look as blank as I felt, and as soon as I thought I was out of his earshot, I said to a friend, "I feel so stupid. I never heard of Corelli!" Of course, there the critic was, still within earshot, and he smiled indulgently to show that my faux pas was not important to him. Not content with making myself a little bit foolish, some demon then made me blab about the blunder to my husband ten minutes later, "Al introduced me to Carl Corelli. I'd never heard of his famous obscure ancestor." As luck would have it, there was Corelli again, and this time he gave me not a forgiving smile but a disbelieving squint.

I know a sophisticated CPA who got into the elevator in her office building. When she saw the company president, her mind went blank—he had shaved off his beard and she didn't recognize him at first. "You look so . . . so . . . young! I mean, well . . . handsome!" Luckily for her, he got off at the next floor and saved her from digging a deeper hole.

Have you ever found yourself coming out with one of the following bloopers?

- ➢ What a pretty baby! What's her name? *Arnold.*
- ➢ Who is that obnoxious person? *My boyfriend.*
- ➢ Are you still dating that strange guy from Minnesota? *We just got married.*
- ➢ You look kind of dragged out. *I just got back from a week at a health spa.*
- ➢ What do you do? *I just lost my job.*

Everybody Blunders

We've all made careless mistakes in conversation. Some are just misguided questions; others are slips of the tongue, or gaffes; and others are innocent but fatal errors like calling your fiancé by an old lover's name. Regardless of who blunders, the victim feels something between amused annoyance and justified outrage, and the culprit feels acute embarrassment; both can be cured only by a genuine apology.

While none of us is immune from blundering, we can all control how we handle it and move on. President George W. Bush was reelected for a second term in spite of his many "Bushisms." He once threw global currency markets into convulsions when he used *devaluation* (loss of value) instead of *deflation* (steadily falling prices) to describe Japanese currency. On another occasion, during a tribute to great woman reformers, he praised Fathi Jahmi, a Libyan dissident, for her advocacy of democracy and free speech—and later realized that Fathi Jahmi is a man. In a conversation with a high-level group of Pentagon officials, he said that "our enemies . . . never stop thinking about new ways to harm our country and our people—and neither do we." His press secretary quickly put that blunder into the most positive light by suggesting that the public empathizes with the difficulty of saying what one means—and so the president's mistakes actually strengthen his bonds with the American people.

Stop Before You Speak

We all find ourselves with a foot in our mouth from time to time. Unless you speak only in the blandest of platitudes, you can't possibly predict ahead of time how other people may be offended by something you say. It can't hurt, though, to slow down and think before you speak. Not only will your precaution save you from sounding silly, but it will protect your friendships from the strain of tactless blurts.

While this advice may seem obvious, many a relationship has been damaged forever by poorly thought-out comments during difficult times or about sensitive subjects. For instance, the pronoun "we" can be pejorative if it suggests that your idea of humanity is limited to people of your skin color, religion, age, or even geographic location, as in "We're a lot more considerate than city people." What seems like a cute joke about trailer parks among well-off friends may backfire when your listener has a brother who could finally afford the little mobile home he'd always dreamed about. Carelessly referring to a newborn who died as "it" can devastate a grieving parent.

Clever humor with people you don't know well can also put your elbow in someone's sore spot. In the novel *Pride and Prejudice,* Elizabeth Bennet teases her new acquaintance, Mr. Darcy, about the potential of teenage girls for mischief. Later she discovers that his innocent young sister came close to being tricked into eloping with a fortune hunter. Elizabeth's wisecracking frightens Mr. Darcy into believing that his sister's private embarrassment is a well-known topic of gossip.

Simply Apologize

Whether you're the one who "dropped a brick," as the English say, or the one on whose foot it landed, there are ways to restore good feeling and get a conversation back in motion. With goodwill and dignity, you can stop making things worse, try to repair blunders, and ask for your trespasses to be forgiven. Whatever you do, try to keep the focus off yourself and your error and on the other person and his importance to you. When you're in a hole, stop digging. Don't stammer, gush, try to rescue the situation with punch lines, or overreact. Even if you are truly embarrassed, don't defend yourself or pass the blame.

Simple apologies are best:

- I'm sorry./I apologize.
- Please forgive me.
- I wasn't thinking.
- I don't know why I said that.
- I'm sorry I said that.
- I goofed; I was stupid.
- That didn't come out the way I meant it.
- Oh, man, just forget I said that.
- Sorry—my mouth just kept talking while my manners went to sleep.

Do not say:

- Hey, just kidding.
- Don't be so sensitive.
- Where's your sense of humor?
- Well, *excuse* me for living!
- Chill out!

Finally, when you apologize for a blunder, skip the melodrama. Only in French can you excuse yourself with apologies like the extravagant "I'm desolated . . ."

If what you have said is truly unforgivable or wounding, and shows bad character, don't demand forgiveness on the spot; you may have to wait until your apology has had time to mellow before the person can grant you forgiveness. Say "I'll understand if you don't want to talk to me for a while; please let me know if you can forgive me someday." Turn to the next chapter for more ways to say "I'm sorry."

How to Respond to Someone Else's Blunder

Happy is he who hears an insult and ignores it:
a hundred evils pass him by.
—Babylonian Talmud: Sanhedrin, c. AD 450

Inevitably, someone says something that really rubs you the wrong way. Before you start to get annoyed, consider the person's nonverbal cues: Does he have mannerisms that already annoyed you, or was the tone of voice the thing that got to you? The timing? The place? Is it just your mood? Some people have a talent for offense, but don't be too ready to see insults when none are intended.

You can't expect people to read your mind or tiptoe around every one of your sensitivities. Ignore small, unintended blunders. Speak up mildly, firmly, and with a smile when you care enough about the person to want him to know that it matters to you. Give a regretful smile and an honest reply: "I'm not sure you'd tell the joke that way if you knew my parents were from Poland."

Give him a chance to retract the comment gracefully, or to clarify what he said: "Are you sure you meant that? My parents were both politicians, and I never once heard of influence peddling."

If a good friend says something hurtful, you probably care enough to respond rather than let it fester. If it is just a stupid blunder by a new acquaintance (someone didn't know you were recently orphaned, for instance), you can comment truthfully but neutrally, move on, and change the topic. Or try something light but definite: "That's a funny way of stereotyping Texans. I may not sound like a Texan, but I'm very loyal to my state." Or "Really? The librarians I know are a pretty lively bunch." Or "Gee, it takes the fun out of being pregnant when people try to scare me with their own fears."

Sometimes, a slow, noncommittal "Oh, I wouldn't say that" is enough to enlighten an ignoramus.

How to Respond When Someone Insults You on Purpose

A soft answer turneth away wrath.
—Proverbs 15:1

Sometimes an insult is uttered on purpose, directed at you personally, prompted by real ugliness, and freighted with ill will. In this case, depending on where you are, you can choose to ignore it or challenge the person—not necessarily on the comment itself or on her character, but on what lies behind the insult. You're probably not going to change the speaker, but you can tell her to stop when you are around.

Possible replies to a thoughtless comment (like a slur against your home state) include:

➤ I'm surprised that you would come out and say that. Have you had a bad experience with Texans?

➤ Well, that's a thought./That's an interesting perspective.

➤ I hear that a lot./I've heard that before./Sure, a lot of people believe that about Texans.

➤ That sounds a little harsh. Have you met a lot of Texans? Have you been to Texas?

➤ It's hard for me not to take that personally.

➤ You seem unhappy enough to risk really offending me.

➤ That's really offensive to Texans.

Even with insults that call for a response, there is no use in taking affronts to heart, even when they may be directed at you personally. Once you have blown your temper, you show lack of trust if the person offended you by accident, or you just put him in a controlling position if the insult was issued on purpose. Don't fight mud with mud. Avoid retorts such as:

> ➤ I'm really upset. You make me so mad.

> ➤ Don't ever say that again.

> ➤ That's so typical of you. I always knew you were a bigot.

> ➤ I can't believe you said that.

> ➤ I knew you didn't like me.

> ➤ Well, you're fat too.

> ➤ Yeah? Well, your mother wears combat boots.

Still, you're not obligated to let someone walk all over you. If someone says something to antagonize you on purpose, whether you smack the insult down or fold it in forgiving phrases, keep your tone level, your attitude bemused, and your expression mild. If the person is worth your while, give her a genuine response. Truth is an absolute defense:

> ➤ I'm interested in that because I am a born-again Christian, and I don't think it applies to all cases. Have you met many born-agains?

> ➤ Not everyone feels that way. Half the kids in my graduating class wanted to do some sort of community service.

> ➤ You must be new around here: gay bashing doesn't get the same automatic laugh after that kid got sued for a hate crime.

Some mean and cloddish comments call for a direct response. Here are some tart rejoinders:

> *It must be boring to be stuck in a little Iowa town.* "Oh, I wouldn't say that. Lots of people have moved here because they like the more civilized pace of life and the lack of snobbery."

> *Another baby? Was she a surprise? Planned? A mistake? Are you Catholics? Mormons? Crazy?* "We're thrilled to have her." "What would make you ask a question like that?" "She means the world to us."

> *(For an adopted baby) Where is his real mother?* "Do you mean his birth mother?" *(For an adopted baby from overseas) What is he?* "What exactly do you mean by that?"

> *She's, you know, one of those people whose names end in a vowel. He's fresh off the boat. They're probably not even legal immigrants.* "Does that kind of thing make a difference to you? I'm married to an Italian myself." "My cousin just became a U.S. citizen."

> *(To any persistent snoop)* "No, I'm really not interested in discussing it. I'm not comfortable saying anything more."

If, in spite of all your self-restraint, the person with whom you are speaking persists in baiting you, don't let his bad manners make you forget your own. If you can't say something polite, just say:

> Could we talk about something else? I find this distasteful.

> I'm uncomfortable with this topic.

> Where is this headed?

Losing your temper rarely produces a good reply to an insult—usually you lose more than you gain. If you feel that irritation is going to make you say something that may lead to long-term damage, you can politely break off the conversation. Give one of the following responses, then leave before you blow your top:

> ➤ I'll let you go on talking about this without me.
> ➤ You'll have to finish this conversation without me.
> ➤ Good-bye.

In the end, kindness may wear down your opponent. Edward Stanton often insulted President Abraham Lincoln and told others that Lincoln was "a low cunning clown . . . the original gorilla." Nevertheless, Lincoln treated Stanton with courtesy and chose him to be his second secretary of war. Even after Stanton assumed this role, he continued to call Lincoln a fool. Once, when word of Stanton's insults got back to the president, Lincoln responded, "Did he call me that? Well, I reckon it must be true then, for Stanton is generally right." The president was able to laugh at his own foibles and take the sting out of Stanton's abuse. When Lincoln died, Stanton called him "the greatest ruler of men the world has ever seen."

ART IS NOT FLAWLESS. Conversation develops a more interesting harmony when you can make something out of the sour notes. Whether you blunder or apologize, or someone else offends you and you don't overreact, you can get the conversation and the connection back on track.

Keep Your Cool

Although sometimes you know ahead of time that a situation or a person will challenge you, you are sometimes caught unprepared. Consider these tactics ahead of time:

- Prepare yourself in advance if you fear that a conversation will make you blow up or break down. If you always cry at an annual performance review, try some of these fixes: promise yourself that you will have a good cry in private as soon as it's over; role-play the situation beforehand with a friend; or write about it in advance to analyze your feelings.

- Develop a mantra, such as "This too will pass" or "I can do this," or count to ten.

- Try to distract yourself from breaking down or blowing up. Imagine the other person in a clown costume, picture a protective shield between yourself and the situation, or imagine yourself on an island where nothing can reach you. Get a cup of water or tea, sit down, or stand up.

- If crying is going to cause professional or personal problems for you—at work, in a meeting, in a crowd of strangers, or when another person needs you for comfort—leave with a promise to return shortly.

- Address underlying issues that may have led to this stressful situation. If you need a sympathetic ear, find one. If you don't feel appreciated, send yourself flowers.

· IV ·

Make Conversations Count

I doubt whether I have ever really talked
to half a dozen persons in my life.
—Nathaniel Hawthorne, 1858

Y OU KNOW THE BASIC FORMAT of a civilized conversation: greet, talk, and finish. This structure is like a trellis on which a conversation grows. Your conversation also will be shaped by where and who you are, your underlying connection with the other person, the context, and how long you talk. You can, of course, say only what the occasion requires, but every conversation offers you the chance to do more, to be creative even in an everyday encounter. In every art, the most ordinary material can still inspire excellence.

In between hello and good-bye, you will often need to say: Please. Thank you. Congratulations (I like what you did). Thank you for the compliment. I don't like what you did. No. I commiserate. I apologize. I accept your apology.

Let's look at several ways to convey these messages with style.

How to Say Please

Ask, and ye shall receive, that your joy may be full.

—John 16:24

Some people have a hard time asking for help. Their reluctance to admit they can't manage on their own makes them defensive. Asking for help does not make you helpless, however; rather, you are helpless if you expect people to read your mind and anticipate your needs. You have to ask. A few years ago, I was struggling with a stroller, a small dog, a howling baby, two shopping bags, a stuck parking meter, and a loose bundle of newspaper, while a teenage boy watched silently from the sidewalk. I burned with resentment that he just stood there watching, but finally, when my shopping bag broke and things started blowing away, I gave up. I took a deep breath, made eye contact with him, and said, "Can you help me? I need an extra hand here." He jumped to attention and replied with a smile, "I thought you'd never ask."

If you need help, be clear and gracious. Don't cringe or flatter. Don't act entitled. Don't act like you expect to be refused. Don't apologize or make excuses.

If you often find it difficult to ask for help, practice asking for small things to learn how to do it when you're really in need. Some people also find it easier to ask for help on behalf of someone else. Either way, you can teach yourself that "please" makes life a lot easier:

➢ Could we squeeze into that seat next to you? My little girl needs to sit in my lap.

➢ I wonder if you could help the cheering section this Friday? Team morale is shaky for this game.

> I don't want to bother you, but I'm late and I can't come back later to pick that up. Could you add it to my order and deliver it?

> Would you be able to pick up Sam from school today?

Ask with courtesy, clarity, and brevity, giving people the option to do something for you that they are probably happy to do. If you feel that someone would like to help somehow and you don't want to put him on the spot, make a bigger and a smaller request at the same time, offering a choice such as "We need help with phoning and with cleanup—could you do either of those?"

Don't ramble on and explain in too much detail why you need something. Don't ask as if you were collecting a debt, enforcing an entitlement, or driving a bargain. Say "Call me whenever I can help you out" or "I hope I can do the same for you someday" *after* you have been helped, not before. Spelling out gratitude up front smacks of deal making, quid pro quo, tit for tat, and an unwillingness to be in anyone's debt even for a moment.

Don't lure the other person into committing to something over and over; make it clear when it is a one-time request.

Do say:

> Do you have five minutes? / I need your help. Is now a convenient time?

> Can you give me some advice?

> Let me tell you about what I need and maybe you can suggest someone who can help me.

> I wonder if you can help me. / Can you do me a favor?

> I thought of you when I needed a special kind of help.

Don't say:

> ➤ I know you don't usually like to do this, but . . .

> ➤ Um, I hate to ask you, but . . .

> ➤ You don't seem busy . . .

> ➤ Somebody ought to . . . /Why don't you . . .

> ➤ Everyone else has given [*x* amount] . . .

Learning to ask for help in a considerate way is good for relationships because it signals your readiness to reciprocate. People who can acknowledge their own needs are often more perceptive about the needs of others. Last year my friend Carol moved from San Francisco into an apartment in a small town, where she soon made a few new acquaintances. Conditioned by big-city anonymity, and busy with work and family, she barely got to know her neighbors on the same floor, even though Mrs. Wu, the lady across the hall from her, had dropped by to leave a bouquet of flowers and introduce herself. Then Carol got sick. She could manage on her own, miserably, but her treatment involved hospital tests that required her to be met and driven home by someone else.

"I cringed to ask, but she was the only person I could think of," Carol admitted to me. Not only did Mrs. Wu drive Carol home, but she offered again, and through the time in the car together, Carol discovered that "not only was she kind and helpful but a truly accomplished conversationalist." When Mrs. Wu moved to a nursing home five years later, Carol was able to be a kind of daughter-on-the-spot to her. By showing herself to be vulnerable, she gave permission for Mrs. Wu to come to her for help. She added, "I don't think we would have gone much beyond hello and welcome if I hadn't asked her for that ride."

Whether you are neighbors, mothers who carpool each other's

children, or strangers who trade help with a tire change for a cup of coffee, asking for something that someone else is happy and able to give can be the basis for a future of many good conversations. People like to help, but first they need to be asked.

How to Say Thank You

Gratitude is not only the greatest of virtues,
but the parent of all others.
—Roman statesman Cicero, 106–43 BC

When you express your gratitude in person, a polite person will probably respond by saying "You're welcome." If you continue with your parade of thanks, she will have to find something else to say, like "Oh, really, it was nothing," or "Anybody would have done the same." Pretty soon you've made her uncomfortable, made her play down the gift, and made your grateful, humble little self the star of the conversation. Don't fawn. People do things for you— give you gifts, offer hospitality, and do favors—not to earn your gratitude and place you under an obligation, but to give you pleasure, warm up the relationship, improve your life, and open up new ways to be connected.

When you say thank you, simply reflect back the kindness that the other person has given to you. Without making other people feel awkward, sometimes you also can widen the spotlight a little in your appreciation. In 1966, Brandeis University awarded the writer John Barth a citation in fiction. He shared the award with Eudora Welty, a writer he greatly admired. Although he began his accept-ance speech lightheartedly with "Not counting Cracker Jacks, this is the first prize of any sort I've won," he ended it graciously by thanking the university in a manner that took the focus off him and moved it onto Ms. Welty: "I thank you kindly for honoring me; I congratulate you heartily for honoring her."

To express your gratitude,

Do say:

➤ Thank you.

➤ Thank you for thinking of me.

➤ It really helped.

➤ I enjoyed it./It made me happy.

➤ It made a big difference.

➤ It's a real honor.

➤ You are so thoughtful.

Don't say:

➤ Now I owe you.

➤ You're so great.

➤ I'm so flattered.

➤ How do I exchange it? It turned out I didn't need it.

➤ I feel terrible for not thanking you./I've been meaning to write you a thank-you note.

No matter how you say it, once you've said thank you in person, the best way to reinforce your gratitude is to write a note of thanks and mail it promptly.

How to Say Congratulations

The deepest principle in human nature is the
craving to be appreciated.

—William James, in a letter to his students at
Radcliffe College, April 6, 1896

Appreciation can take two forms: "Thank you for what you did for me" and "I congratulate you for what you've accomplished." Recognition and admiration are called for when a person earns a new academic degree or a promotion at work, runs a marathon, shows her art in an exhibit, or has a new baby. Look for opportunities to congratulate people without making them uncomfortable. Here are some ways to give and to accept compliments in turn.

I Like What You Did

When someone has had a success, keep the conversation off yourself for a while. Sometimes, even when you're trying to offer the kindest kudos, you have to suppress your own feelings of jealousy and inadequacy. Ask questions and let her talk; don't compare her achievement with your own or anyone else's. Avoid the slightest hint of envy. Don't try to sidle into her spotlight or turn one on yourself.

In the film *Casablanca,* the characters Rick Blaine and Victor Laszlo were both in love with the same woman, and they had every reason to envy each other. Still, one was able to compliment the other respectfully and without a trace of jealousy:

RICK: *I congratulate you.*

VICTOR: *What for?*

RICK: *Your work.*

VICTOR: *I try.*

RICK: *We all try. You succeed.*

An awkward compliment is worse than no compliment at all. A prepubescent boy was raised to always tell the truth, and at his first dance he also was instructed by his mother to compliment his partner. Laboring to reconcile these two demands, he finally came up with "For a fat girl, you don't sweat much." Nobody likes to hear "You look really good for your age" or "I wish my wife had a mini-career like yours" or "You have such a cute little apartment." When you congratulate someone you actually envy, beware of handing her a gift-wrapped insult instead.

When you wish to make a considerate compliment,

Do say:

➤ Congratulations.

➤ That is great news.

➤ You deserve this./You deserve each other.

➤ This makes everyone around you so happy. You must be so pleased.

➤ You must be so proud of [a successful relative/a team member].

➤ We're happy for you.

Don't say:

➤ I hate you for being so thin./I wish it were me.

➤ You have such luck./I guess some people have all the luck.

➤ I did that once.

- ➤ Are you still going to talk to average people like us?

- ➤ You're stupendous.

- ➤ I'm so proud of you. (This suggests you had a hand in his success. Don't act like the stage mom behind a friend's achievement.)

Artwork calls for a particular kind of compliment. One of the biggest steps an amateur artist takes is to understand the word *amateur*. It means "one who loves," but what is loved and admired is the art, not the artist. Always separate the two.

Do say:

- ➤ That is my favorite painting in the show.

- ➤ I love your new electric guitar solos. Your music has changed a lot in two years.

- ➤ I've enjoyed seeing your work develop over the years.

- ➤ I liked the surprise in the second act of that play.

- ➤ This has me thinking about landscape in a whole new way.

These specific and authentic compliments show the artist that you have paid attention to his work, and he can thank you genuinely rather than pretend false modesty. They are preferable to empty phrases like:

- ➤ Your work is the most, the best, one of a kind, most unique . . .

- ➤ It's great./I love it!

- ➤ You're the most famous dancer in the city.

- ➤ You have so much talent. / You're so famous. / You're so great. / You're so fabulous.
- ➤ You must be getting rich off your art.

I Like This Person You Created

Just as you can congratulate an artist for his work, you can compliment new parents on the new baby they created or brought into the family. This type of compliment, however, calls for special tact. While to their parents they look like angels, most new babies look like tiny, wrinkled, disapproving, newly awakened, unwilling visitors from a different world.

After my editor's daughter was born, she joked, "I decided from then on I would tell every brand-new mother that her baby looked just like her around the eyes or the nose or that they had the same mouth. Who can tell, really? And I remember how happy it made me to hear it."

Use the baby's name when you admire him or her, and try to find something nice to say that shows you care about the parents' joy:

Do say:

- ➤ What a pretty baby!/That's a beautiful baby.
- ➤ What a fine baby./What a handsome little guy.
- ➤ How are you doing?
- ➤ I'll bet you are really happy.
- ➤ She looks like both of you—she's got your eyes and her dad's mouth.
- ➤ How is she sleeping? (and either congratulate or commiserate)

Don't say:

➤ What's wrong with his nose?/Should he be that color?/Isn't he awfully small?

➤ Shouldn't you be breast-feeding?

➤ Did you want a boy?

➤ Is he a good baby?

➤ He looks like Churchill!/She looks like ET!

➤ It's really cute. (If you really can't tell the gender, lead off with "You've got a really cute baby there. How old?")

When you visit a family with a newborn, congratulate the older child and spend time with him. Build him up a little—his ego may have taken a hit.

Do say:

➤ The baby is almost as cute as you.

➤ This means you are a big brother.

➤ Does the baby have a lot to say?

➤ That baby is lucky to have you for a big brother.

➤ I remember when you were just born.

Don't:

➤ Exaggerate either positives or negatives about the family's new addition.

➤ Fawn over the baby when her sibling is around.

➤ Bad-mouth the baby as a nuisance.

➤ Say "I bet you're jealous."

How to Receive a Compliment

I can live for two months on a good compliment.

—Mark Twain, 1835–1910

The flip side of offering warm congratulations is accepting another person's admiration gracefully. A special kind of thank-you is called for when someone gives you a compliment. Keep the focus where the person intended—on making you feel good.

Do say "Thank you" and then add something that puts the conversation back in play:

➤ I got it when I went to the Wisconsin State Fair.

➤ It was a gift from my grandmother when I was still a tomboy. It was my first piece of real jewelry.

➤ I love the color too. This color is called punk purple— amazing how they name these things, isn't it?

➤ Thanks. My haircut still surprises me when I look in the mirror. It must be the way a man feels when he shaves off his beard.

➤ Thanks for the compliment. My toddler said, "Mommy, those glasses make you look like a bug."

➤ Thanks, she's worked hard to learn the violin. She would love to hear that from you firsthand. (Teach that kid to handle a compliment too!)

➤ (and to a close friend) Thanks. It actually cost less than lunch at our favorite restaurant.

If you are an artist of any kind, learn to accept compliments about your work as being distinct from compliments to you personally. Then you and the person making the compliment can regard the work together with real appreciation, and talk about what went into it with some distance and perspective, much as you appreciate the success of a friend or family member. You can respond to a person's praise of your work with:

> Thanks, I do this because I love to do it, but it is so nice to get encouragement.

> I'm glad you think so.

> I hope you enjoyed looking at it as much as I enjoyed creating it.

When you receive a compliment, don't pretend to be unworthy or respond with a negative like: "It's as old as the hills." "It was cheap." "Anyone could have done it." What you have or what you have accomplished may be something that the other person aspires to—don't denigrate his dream.

Don't say:

> Oh, you're just being nice. This old thing?

> Aw, shucks.

> Oh, it's nothing. I'm no good at shopping. I never know what to get you.

> Well, I like what you're wearing too.

> You don't really mean that.

> You're too kind.

> I've worn it ten times before and no one noticed it.

> (to someone you don't know well) It was a bargain./It only cost me twenty dollars.

How to Say "I Don't Like What You Did"

Aunt March possessed, in perfection, the art of rousing the spirit of opposition in the gentlest people, and enjoyed doing it.
—Louisa May Alcott, *Little Women*, 1868

Giving and receiving compliments is a pleasure compared to the opposite: dishing out and responding to criticism. Nevertheless, sometimes the two sides of this coin are complementary: your timing and your skill at offering focused compliments can be an asset when you need to express a complaint or a criticism. "I love you in blue, but that outfit isn't as flattering as the flower dress" works better, an hour before the party, than "Those pants make you look fat" once you get there. Prefacing a negative comment with a positive one can help you put whatever is bothering you in proper perspective, and often it shrinks a crime to a misdemeanor before you even bring it up. Praise can soften requests, too, as in "You did a nice job on the kitchen, but we still have to bring in the groceries." You'd be surprised how well this works, even with teenagers and perfectionists.

How to Criticize with Civility

You've got to accentuate the positive, eliminate the negative, and latch on to the affirmative. Don't mess with Mister In-between!
—Johnny Mercer, "Ac-Cent-Tchu-Ate the Positive," 1944

When you must tell someone that something is bothering you or if you want to offer constructive criticism, mention only that which a person can take action to change (preferably right away). For example: "You've left your shirt untucked in the back," not "Why didn't you buy better shirts?"

Also, consider speaking in terms of sound rather than visuals, as in: "You usually sound so upbeat. What's got you down tonight?" rather than "Why the long face?"

When you have something critical to say, don't preface it with a lot of squeamish apologies; you'll just turn a routine bit of information into a weirdly loaded topic. Stop before issuing any statement that begins "I hate to say this, but . . ." "I hope you'll forgive my mentioning it, but . . . ," or "No offense, but . . ." And harping on how uncomfortable it makes you to offer useful criticism will just keep the focus on you and your discomfort, not the person and your concern for his well-being.

Last, always distinguish your feelings about the person from what he or she is doing: "I love you, but I don't like the way you shout at your little brother," or "I care about you both, and it makes me uncomfortable to hear about your private disagreements."

How to Respond to Constructive Criticism

I disagree with what you say, but I defend your right to say it.
—Voltaire, 1694–1778

It's easy to make good conversation when you're surrounded by friends, enjoying a gathering, and buoyed up by a fascinating topic. One of the acid tests of civilized conversation, however, is how you respond to criticism and negativity.

Many people can't gracefully handle even a constructive comment, such as "Your soup would taste better with a little more salt." Handling constructive criticism may bring out your irrationality; sometimes you may feel that you would agree with what the person is saying if you didn't have to admit that he had the right to say it. It's almost easier to handle a disagreement than to keep your cool when you've been criticized, fairly, for something you can change.

Criticism is easier to accept if you break it into two parts: acknowledge that you heard it, and take the appropriate action. It doesn't cost you anything to say that you appreciate his concern, whether you agree with his suggestion or not, and whether you think it's any of his business or not. You can then fix it if you agree, or not if you don't. To hear is not always to obey, but just saying "I hear you" sounds good enough for a lot of people.

Use one of these phrases in your acquiescence:

➤ Thanks, I hadn't noticed that yet.

➤ That's good advice.

➤ Thanks, you saved me a lot of [trouble, embarrassment, money, anxiety].

➤ I'm glad you pointed it out.

➤ I agree.

➤ Got it.

➤ I have it that way on purpose, but I value your input.

Don't say:

➤ No, it isn't.

➤ Don't tell me how to run my life.

➤ You're always criticizing me.

If a person *is* always criticizing you, just develop a water-off-a-duck's-back response that lets her feel she's been heard, without your always having to take action. When asked how she copes with criticism, the celebrity Paris Hilton said, "I tell people what they want to hear and then I do what I want to do."

How to Say No

Too much agreement kills a chat.
—Eldridge Cleaver, *Soul on Ice*, 1968

Someone once said, "Stress is when your mouth says yes and your gut says no." Being civilized isn't the same as being evasive or mealy-mouthed, or saying yes when you really mean no. You probably spend your time with people who care enough about you to pay attention when you say what you mean, even when you have trouble saying what that is. What you do say and don't say, and how you say it, can keep the conversation civilized when you have to say no.

You don't have to refuse reasonable requests, such as "For the last time, would you clean up your room!" or "Can you help me? I've just been robbed!" Many unreasonable requests, however, come smiling up to you sounding reasonable, fooling you into agreement. For example, people often ask you to do something you don't want to do and that you are not responsible for in the normal course of things—baby-sit, volunteer, make phone calls, give a talk, eat a second helping, have another drink, meet them at the last minute. Good manners do not require it. You know you don't have enough time to do the job well. And if you're really honest with yourself, you know you'll resent it if you say yes. From "Spare change?" to "Would you be our chairman?," you sometimes have to decline people's requests.

When you have to say no, do say "No, thank you" or "No," and back it up with one of the following phrases:

Short and Sweet

➢ I just can't.

➢ Thank you so much for thinking of me, but I can't possibly do it.

{ 114 }

I'm Already Committed

➤ (In business) I'm not taking on any new tasks/projects this [year/month]./My boss (or agent) wouldn't be happy if I took that on.

➤ My lawyer or my accountant or my family won't let me. (And teenagers, memorize these five magic words: "My mom would kill me.")

➤ If I say yes now, I'd still let you down later.

➤ I'm already spread a little too thin. My in-box is full.

I Have Physical Limitations

➤ I'm allergic./I had some and it was delicious./I've already had seconds.

➤ This was perfect.

➤ I don't drink. No, really, I can't drink. It disagrees with me./One is my limit.

What's the Reward?

➤ Do you have a budget? (Will I be paid?)

➤ Will my name be in the program (and be spelled correctly)?

➤ (When freelancing) I can do that, but I'd have to turn down another job. (This signals that your professional time is not free.)/I can meet your deadline, but I'd have to charge extra for the rush job.

Here's Another Solution

➤ I'd rather be a committee member than a chairman (or vice versa).

➤ I can't do that, but I can do something else (donate something, give money, phone, attend).

➤ I can do it next semester.

➤ I'm not the best person for that job. Why don't you try Ms. Wannadoo? (And be sure that this person will not hit the roof or duck the job.)

Don't say:

➤ I don't know. I'll think about it. Maybe. Beg me. Well, okay. Yes.

➤ Let someone else do it.

➤ I'd love to do it [if your inner self is screaming NO].

➤ I've already done more than my share.

When you say no, don't explain, apologize, or elaborate. Just pleasantly but firmly stick to your refusal. Don't add more excuses.

When people pressure you to help them at the last minute, think of this message I once saw in a post office: "Your lack of planning is not a personal emergency for me." You don't have to say it out loud, but it will remind you of your right to say no.

How to Say "I Commiserate"

There is no man . . . that imparteth his griefs to his friends, but he grieveth less.

—Francis Bacon, *Essays*, 1601

It's far from a perfect world; the lives of the people around you are dotted with disasters large and small. Your friends may be going through a divorce or a breakup; coping with an illness (either of their own or in their family); struggling with work or school; moving; recovering from a theft, fire, car accident, or scandal; or agonizing over a child's difficulties. Always leave the conversational door open, but don't assume they want to walk through it every time they see you. Just be available.

Offer a sympathetic opener that lets them choose whether they want to acknowledge the problem and talk about it. For example, "I haven't seen you for a while; how are you doing?" or "How are things now?" or "I don't know if you want to talk about what happened" or "I heard about what happened at work, but you may not want to talk about it yet."

People vary widely in their responses. Some will be relieved to acknowledge that they have a problem; others cope better by keeping it to themselves.

When a person in trouble is ready to talk about it, it's best not to say anything that turns the focus to yourself.

Don't say:

➢ I know how you feel.

➢ It's awful. I'm so upset over this. I'm heartbroken.

➢ The same thing happened to me, only worse.

➢ I don't know what to say.

➢ Why didn't you call me?

➢ I was too upset to call.

➢ You must be devastated/crushed/really mad. . . .

No matter what kind of disaster your friends are facing, don't act more upset over their lives than they are.

The People You Meet: The Complainer

Three grandmothers sat down together: The first one said, "Oy."
The second one said, "Oy veh." The third one said, "I thought we
agreed not to talk about the grandchildren."

The common everyday complainer may be in a bad mood because she is having a rough day, going through a divorce, ticked off at her boss, flunking a class, or on a deadline. The next person she runs into—you—gets an earful, and then she feels better. You sympathize because you've had days like that and you know she will be back to usual when the problem gets resolved.

The chronic complainer, however, doesn't seem to feel better no matter how much she complains. She is happy only when she is miserable. Wedded to her troubles, she prefers self-pity to your pity, and will argue back when you try to cheer her up. Sometimes she actually likes to hang out with others who confirm her gloomy view of the world.

If you listen sympathetically to the chronic complainer today, tomorrow she'll be back with a fresh complaint, or sometimes even the same one all over again. Try as you may, you never feel that she gets any cheer from the sunshine you try to bring into her life. In the book *I'm OK, You're OK*, Thomas Harris characterized this person as the "ain't it awful" type. She always seems to be in a bad mood about something. Every doughnut has a hole in it; every silver lining has a cloud; everyone is having fun but her. When she greets you with gloom, she sounds like Eeyore the dismal donkey: "Good morning, Pooh Bear. If it is a good morning, which I doubt."

Sometimes a chronic complainer really just wants to inflate her own achievements by focusing on all the difficulties she faces. At other times, it's simple narcissism. When confronted with a complainer, don't argue, don't offer advice or solutions, and don't oversympathize. You almost don't have to say much, because just listening is enough. The one thing you can do is monitor whether she is telling you things that she should not—about someone she's mad at or some insecurity of her own.

How to Say "I Apologize"

I'm sorry. I'm sorry. I'm sorry. I said I was sorry three times.
—Blanche DuBois, character in *A Streetcar Named Desire*, 1951

It's hard enough to comfort someone who is suffering. It's infinitely harder when you caused her pain. We all make mistakes, but we don't all know how to apologize gracefully. A concern about lawsuits has caused some people to apologize less or to offer lukewarm, passive apologies like "Mistakes were made." Even in court, however, guilty people who say "I'm sorry for what I did" to the victim or the victim's family receive more lenient sentences and ultimately earlier parole than those who don't.

To make amends when you've hurt someone, take the following steps:

1. First, find out what actually happened as a result of your mistake. Don't assume right away that you are either at fault or not at fault. Don't underreact or overreact.

2. Determine how much responsibility you bear.

3. Apologize in person. If you just can't face it, apologize by phone or write a note by hand first and make sure it

reaches the offended party right away; then apologize in person *too*. Express the hope that this mistake will not end the friendship.

4. Ask but don't beg to be forgiven; ask for forgiveness to come later if the person seems very hurt.

5. Offer restitution. Find out if there is anything you can do to repair the damage.

6. Wait and let time do some of the healing. Don't keep apologizing, but do show that you haven't forgotten.

7. Never make that mistake again.

It's always uncomfortable to apologize, but don't talk about your own feelings as a way to weasel out of accepting responsibility for hurts that you inflict, especially when the other person is already struggling. Don't expect the person you have hurt to sympathize with your discomfort. In the early 1990s, when AIDS transmission was still poorly understood, the mother of one healthy fifth grader asked forgiveness from the mother of an afflicted child for not letting these former best friends play together any longer. She said, "I'm brokenhearted over having to do this." The second mother replied, "No, *I'm* brokenhearted; you're just uncomfortable."

To express your remorse,

Do say:

➤ I am so sorry. / Please forgive me. / I need your forgiveness.

➤ I apologize.

➤ I didn't mean to . . . but I did.

➤ Can I help with the medical expenses/cleaning bill/cost of repair?

> I can understand if you can't forgive me now. I hope someday you will be able to.

Don't say:

Anything that turns the focus back to yourself:

> I feel terrible. I'm a terrible person./I'm upset.

> You're mad at me. Don't be mad./What's the matter? I said I was sorry!

Anything that makes the harm seem passive:

> I'm sorry if I caused any pain (and not sorry about anything I can deny).

> I'm sorry for anything I might have done.

> I was just joking. Can't you see the humor in it?

Anything that negates your apology:

> It wasn't my fault. Someone else made me do it.

> I'm sorry, but . . .

And never use e-mail to apologize.

How to Accept an Apology

For to be social is to be forgiving.
—Poet Robert Frost, "The Star-Splitter," 1920s

When someone sincerely apologizes to you, be approachable and courteous. Make eye contact. A Muslim cleric said, "A person courageous enough to apologize for his errors is worthy of praise." Even if you cannot forget what the person has done, acknowledge the courage that was required for him to ask for your forgiveness. Forgiveness will free you to move forward. Refusing to accept an apology will only lead to ill feelings that may come back to haunt you when you are the one who must ask for forgiveness in the future.

Whether you're on the giving or receiving end of forgiveness, congratulations, or criticism, you can transform common conversations into thoughtful exchanges. Ordinary materials don't have to limit your creativity. Adding some art to simple words like "please," "thank you," "no," and "I'm sorry" can help you change everyday conversations into genuine communication.

· V ·

Change Situations into Conversations

Now is the time for conversation.

—Ovid, *The Art of Love*, 1 BC

CONVERSATION doesn't take place in a vacuum. You move from office water cooler to post office line to soccer carpool to church coffee hour, talking all the time. You can connect appropriately wherever you find yourself if you pay attention to how people talk in different situations.

Each situation imposes limits: how many other people are present, how well you know one another, the length of the encounter, and the underlying agenda. You wouldn't talk about business at a wedding reception, nor would you tell intimate family stories on a crowded elevator. A stranger's hello at a friend's baby shower elicits a different response from a stranger's hello on the subway, and the questions that you might ask an acquaintance if you run across him or her in the doctor's waiting room are different from the kind you might ask while waiting for a committee meeting to start.

Each place offers opportunities: you can discover things about another person, explore new ideas, make the most of an event, and learn about yourself. New settings can turn strangers into new acquaintances, acquaintances into friends, and new friends into close friends. When you meet one of your mother's friends at a political fundraiser, you may both end up finding new facets of yourselves, the world, and each other. You're no longer bound by your role as her friend's son and her role as your mother's friend; rather, you have a different stage, cast of characters, and drama to enact. You may see a different side of someone from your carpool when you go bowling together. You'll choose different things to talk about; the person will hear you in a different way.

Don't avoid piping up in new settings, but welcome the chance to hear a new part of each person's story—and to tell your own. Here is a guide to help you make something uncommon out of common, everyday encounters.

During a Chance Encounter

Never try to say something remarkable. It is sure to be wrong.
—Mark Rutherford, *Last Pages from a Journal*, 1915

Whether you're on the street or at a high school reunion, it's great to run across someone you know or used to know. With some acquaintances, you can pick up right where you left off, regardless of whether a week or a year has passed since you last met. With others, however, the conversation calls for a little kick-starting to get over the fact that you've been out of touch, or to help both of you collect your wits and get the friendship back up to speed.

Do:

➢ Supply your name readily, just in case he has forgotten. If the encounter is really out of context, his memory may need a jog.

➢ Stick to general conversational openers at first: "Great to see you." "How have you been?" "How is your family?"

➢ Express fondness for the person and perhaps recall a positive shared experience: "I've thought of you often." "I thought of you last week when I heard that song we both liked."

➢ Be ready, but don't demand to be introduced to his or her companions.

Don't:

➢ Be defensive and pretend that you should have been in touch. Don't make elaborate excuses. (Simply acknowledge the pleasure of seeing the person and resume your acquaintance.)

➢ Attach blame to yourself or the other person because of the lull in your relationship: "I've been too busy to call" or "You never return my calls. You've been avoiding me."

➢ Say "I wouldn't have recognized you."

➢ Zero in too fast on specifics you remember about the last time you saw him or her. You risk hitting a sore topic or exposing how distant the acquaintance really is.

➢ Use the phrase "Are you still . . ." It can be demeaning to an artist who takes her work seriously to be asked "Are you still painting?" Would you ask a doctor "Are you still a doctor?" Use another construction: "What are you painting now?" or "What's new in your work life?" "What are you working on now?"

High school and college reunions are like a world unto themselves when it comes to conversation. Standing in back of (and sometimes in front of) each person is the younger person frozen in time. It takes a few minutes of conversation in the here and now to warm up the connection so those ghosts can melt.

Don't jump in with how you felt about that person—that would be like telling a teenager how you remember him as a child. "I had the biggest crush on you" may not be something the person who doesn't even remember you wants to hear. Even favorable comparisons can blow up in your face. A backhanded compliment like "You used to be such a nerd and now you're so successful" may be like a stiletto between the ribs of a high-tech CEO who still has high school insecurities just below the surface.

In the Elevator

That was a very small room.

—Peter Sellers as Chance the gardener, who had never ridden on an elevator, in the film *Being There*, 1979

An elevator ride provides the opportunity for a tiny, fleeting group event; you and one other person or a few people have something in common for ten to sixty seconds. You may encounter people you know as well as people you don't know (or they may recognize you and know who you are, even if you don't know them). In such close contact, it's best to keep conversation generic.

Do:

➢ Show respect for the other person's physical and personal space.

➢ Make brief eye contact with other people.

➢ Transcend the potential for a minute of torment by

Polish Your Conversational Skills

We are presented with endless opportunities for practicing civilized conversational skills. Doing so when you are less invested in an outcome will make you feel more at ease in situations when you are more self-conscious.

- Coming out of your shell is easier if you practice. If you usually go through your day with your head down, lost in thought, begin by noticing the people around you. Practice your friendly smile and hello on the girl behind the counter at the coffee shop.

- Move to striking up conversations with people you see regularly but probably know very little about, like the dry cleaner or your child's teacher at school. These don't have to be intimate, probing conversations, but you can make a friendly connection with a question about their holiday plans or vacation.

- The next time you are at a large family event with people you may not know so well, make an effort to get to know them better. You can talk to the same people you always do because it is easy and you have so much in common, or you can use the occasion to establish bonds among the larger family unit.

- Reach out to your neighbors or coworkers. Instead of a wave or a nod, ask them how their day is going or if they noticed the new shop that opened on the corner.

- Invite people over or go to lunch and pay attention to the finer points of how the conversation moves so that when you are in a higher-risk situation, like your boss's cocktail party, you will be confident.

making the elevator chat positive and uplifting. At least nod, smile, or say hello.

➤ Recognize that some people aren't ready for a full-blown conversation in an elevator.

Don't:

➤ Perpetuate inane sayings like "Thank God it's Friday!"

➤ Stare at people after making initial eye contact. Instead, face nearly forward, even when conversing.

➤ Share private information about your business, customers, patients, family, or self.

➤ Repeatedly push the elevator buttons as if you can't wait to get out (and away from the other person).

➤ Assume that people you encounter on the elevator want to continue the conversation beyond the ride.

If you strike up a conversation in an elevator, don't use the opportunity of having a captive audience to make an "elevator pitch" to promote your business or religious beliefs to complete strangers. Doing so is an act of aggression—like a telemarketing call someone can't hang up on.

If a slight acquaintance asks you what you've been up to, briefly sum up your latest project. When the ride is over, ask if he or she would like to hear more about it sometime with statements like: "I know you're in a business related to what I'm doing. Is this something you'd like to hear more about?" or "I'll go on if you want to know more about this." Respect the fact that he may be busy and may not want to hear more than what you have to say during the elevator ride.

If you ride the elevator a few times each day in an office building, prepare yourself for the eventuality of encountering your boss or your boss's boss there. It never hurts to have a few topics in mind in advance.

On the Bus or in the Bleachers

The time to stop talking is when the other person nods his head affirmatively but says nothing.
—Henry Stanley Haskins, *Meditations on Wall Street,* 1940

From time to time, we all find ourselves sitting beside strangers on a bus, train, or airplane, or sharing a row of seats in a sports stadium or a concert hall. In these situations, making friends is not the main agenda, but an acquaintanceship can begin between two people who share the same space and the same experience for longer than a few minutes, especially if season tickets or a daily commute is involved.

No doubt, throughout your life you will sit next to many people who make moderately interesting conversation. Only rarely, however, do seatmates become soul mates. In the best instances, you will greet each other politely, find common interests, and chat a bit. When the time is up, you will part with good wishes or find a way to follow up. In other cases, you will need more skill to converse. One of you may want to talk more than the other, or you may not find any common interests at all. When you talk with people sitting next to you:

Do:

➤ Respect your fellow passenger's interest or lack of interest in conversing. Stay alert for signals that he or she may prefer to sleep or read.

- Speak loudly enough to be heard by the person next to you, but quietly enough so that you don't disturb people in front of you and behind you.

- Be courteous, but reserved. If you're ready to wrap up the conversation after a few minutes, say "I usually read on trips like this. Maybe we could talk later."

- Moderate your initial enthusiasm or dislike if you will be seated next to this person again. Keep the conversation low-key and avoid hot buttons. Let the relationship develop, if it will, slowly.

Don't:

- Lean over to read something that another passenger is reading.

- Make eye contact unless you are open to a few minutes' conversation.

- Pursue conversation beyond the setting until you find out more about the person. One often finds that there is about one hour's worth of interest, and not much more, on a two-and-a-half-hour ride. You can receive a business card or phone number without offering yours. Just politely say "I can call you" to signal that you will decide if the acquaintanceship is to continue.

- Let caution spoil the conversation. Enjoy the moment without any concern that you're getting yourself into a long-term commitment.

- Mistake the shared elation or despair over a football game for a warm friendship.

- Talk loudly on a cell phone.

Take cues from your own feelings, the other person, and the situation that you find yourself in before you decide whether and how to proceed with a conversation. If you're not comfortable, don't keep talking. If you are comfortable, you may find that this transient connection can lead to something more.

In a Waiting Room

The real art of conversation is not only to say the right thing in the right place, but to leave unsaid the wrong thing at the tempting moment.

—Lady Dorothy Nevill, socialite, 1826–1913

Some settings can lead you into conversational quicksand, where you risk being dragged down by topics that are best avoided. The waiting room in the office of a doctor, therapist, lawyer, or principal can present such challenges. So can public lounges in a police station, courthouse, or office building.

It's hard not to blurt "What's wrong?" when you meet someone you know in the doctor's waiting room, or "Who are you waiting to see?" "What are you doing here?" in the dean's office, or "I hope nothing's wrong" in a legal office. Even someone who is waiting to get good news may not want to talk about it at the moment you ask.

Do say:

➤ Hello.

➤ How nice to see you. How have you been?/How nice to run into you. (This lets the person decide what he or she wants to talk about.)

➤ We have the same clinic. How nice. (Don't get too specific.)

Be very sensitive to polite evasion. If you have asked a blunt question and gotten a vague answer, don't keep asking.

Don't:

➤ Ask a fellow patient about the purpose of his visit or which doctor he is going to see.

➤ Tie up the receptionist in conversation if he is busy.

➤ Lament a third person's condition.

➤ Offer details about your reasons for being there. Let the other person ask, and even then you don't have to say more than you are comfortable with. "I have a routine checkup" is always a good nonreply; "I'm catching up on some details" is about as nondescript as you can get. You don't owe anyone information that you don't want to provide.

➤ Pass on to the next person you see that you ran into your friend at such an office—sometimes it's enough to get a rumor started.

At a Coffee Hour or a Cocktail Hour

Flee not from conversation.
—Ovid, *The Art of Love,* 1 BC

Many meetings, religious services, parent-teacher conferences, and performances include an informal social hour, with or without food, where people can catch up with existing acquaintances or make new friends.

One benefit of supporting arts groups is that sometimes you are invited to meet the artists—to mingle with the poets, painters, dancers, musicians, singers, writers, and actors who actively make their living in the heady world of the creative arts. You have the chance to hear their opinions and find out more about their lives—and often you discover that they have the same ordinary conversational problems we all have. I was enchanted when a virtuoso violinist told me, "I love coming to these parties and meeting people who do something else—anything other than music—for a living. Musicians get so tired of hanging out with each other and talking shop."

Do:

➤ Compliment the speaker or performer briefly. Find one detail from the sermon, homily, speech, or performance that made an impression on you. But don't reprise the whole thing just to show you were listening.

➤ Circulate and help people meet one another.

➤ Greet people standing alone who look like they don't know anyone.

➤ Introduce yourself to anyone you might like to meet.

Don't:

➤ Try to have a quick committee meeting or a long personal conversation.

➤ Criticize the program excessively. You can say "I am going to have to think about what he said" rather than "What a load of nonsense!" or "Borrrring!" You never know when you might be talking to a fan or a relative of the speaker or performer.

➤ Monopolize the speaker with an in-depth discussion or a description of your work as it relates to what he does.

Arrange to get in touch later if you really want to pursue a fuller conversation.

➤ Swarm all over a newcomer. Sometimes people visit around a bit to see what group they feel at home with. Be warm and welcoming, but give them time to get acquainted before you assume they're ready to join.

○ ○ ○

The People You Meet: The Drinker

Whatever the Persians discuss when sober, is always a second time examined after they have been drinking.
—Herodotus, *The Histories*, c. 430 BC

While drinking has accompanied conversations and happy occasions for thousands of years, it has always carried the risk of excess. A temporary mind-fuzz comes when a person drinks too much. Don't expect much from a conversation in which at least one person has consumed too much of something that both removes her inhibitions and depresses her emotions.

If the inebriated person says things that offend you, don't take the specifics to heart. Keep the discussion simple, don't argue, and look around for help from the person's companion or someone who can take over if she gets unstable. Take all romantic talk with a grain of salt when you hear it from a drunk.

Don't hold her drinking against her. Social pressures push people to drink while they talk and to believe that drinking will help them talk better.

If you notice someone who routinely drinks too much and says things you know he will regret, don't fail to let him know the next day that while you don't take it personally, you are concerned that he drank so much. Be a truth-teller rather than a silent accomplice. If you feel that your friendship will sustain it, you can try to talk about the problem with an offer of help, insight, or experience—but only if you have been there yourself or with a relative. Even then, don't assume that the person will want to talk with you in ordinary conversation about his drinking habits.

At a Sit-down Dinner

People who take a wait-and-see attitude I could kill; they spoil it for everyone. A wonderful guest is one who doesn't sit on the edge watching. A wonderful guest is someone who charms, who communicates—who, in short, really wants to be there.

—Kate Medina, Doubleday editor, quoted in Emile Jean Pin, *The Pleasure of Your Company*, 1985

Adult social life is more fun if you can enjoy leisurely conversation with all types of people over good food. Bear in mind that the food is the pretext, not the reason, for the gathering; good table manners are absolutely vital; and drinking, eating, or talking too much is never attractive.

Do:

➢ Go around and meet people before dinner, and, if possible, don't limit yourself to knowing just your two dinner partners. Talk to as many fellow guests at your table as possible, and help keep your conversation open to all. If possible, introduce yourself to everyone who will be sitting

Be the Best Host

A formal or informal gathering is a wonderful way to bring people together. The host is the person who makes the event a success by careful and thoughtful planning.

- Choose your guests wisely. For the best conversations, invite people who have more in common than just the fact that they know you. Mix talkers and listeners.

- Invite your guests well in advance to avoid any implication that they are on your B-list or they don't have much to do but wait for your invitation to brighten their life. When you invite friends to come over, don't make them accept your invitation without knowing what they are in for. Don't say: What are you doing tonight?/Are you busy next Saturday?/If you're not doing anything . . ./We owe you dinner. Never invite someone to an event in front of someone who isn't invited.

- Set the stage. Tell your guests what is planned and who will be there. Don't make them fish for important information—for example, that it's BYOB, Dutch treat, Halloween costume, grown-ups only, or girls only.

- Your job is to help your guests connect with one another. Don't spend all of your effort cooking and serving while your guests struggle with half-heard names, grope for common interests, and go home without meeting the person they would have enjoyed most!

around the table, even those who may be too far away to talk with during the meal.

➤ Give equal time to the people on your left and your right.

➤ Talk across the table if it's less than three feet wide and you can hear each other clearly.

➤ Ask the host whom you ought to introduce yourself to.

➤ Show appreciation for whatever efforts are made on your behalf. Sometimes it's nice to propose a toast to the hosts so that everyone can thank them.

Don't:

➤ Monopolize another guest's time or dominate the whole table's dinner conversation.

➤ Monopolize the host, especially in the early stages of a dinner party. Intense private conversation with you may distract him from his other guests.

➤ Automatically call the next day to thank the host and talk some more. You just spent the evening together, didn't you, and thanked her when you left? Instead, promptly send a handwritten note to underscore your gratitude. (See chapter IX).

○ ○ ○

The People You Meet: The Appraiser

Appraisers measure others' usefulness by their academic position, their address, their club memberships, their proximity to government power, their profession, their income, their access to money, their marital status, their family connections, or their car. A seemingly innocent conversational opener, such as "What do you do?" "Where did you go to school?" or "Are you married?" can mask a hidden quest to find out how the listener can use you.

This once happened to a colleague of mine. He said, "I thought I'd found a real friend when I joined my tennis group. The wife of one of the guys, Carla Grabbe, I'll call her, was interested in everything about me: my kids, my job, and my neighborhood. When my father was sick, she always asked how he was doing, and then when he died she sent the nicest card. I did kind of wonder what she found so interesting about me, but I always enjoyed her attentions and the feeling that she was on my side.

"Well, like most things that seem too good to be true, it was. The month after my dad died, she hit me with it: 'You ought to be thinking of a move to a bigger house.' She was a real estate agent and she saw me as a potential client who had probably inherited some money. Now I'm careful to get into friendships where I do my share right away, finding out about the other person, asking about their interests and their life, rather than just feeling lucky to have someone else putting the energy in."

It can be profoundly disappointing to find that someone you thought was a friend has been storing you up to do something useful for her. Be realistic about settings where you may meet people with this kind of agenda. For instance, the central purpose of a networking cocktail party, fundraising gala for an organization, political salon, mixer, alumni reception, or election rally is not the adventure of getting to know a person better through conversation, but about figuring out ways to leverage people's positions, knowledge, and power. And if you don't measure up—if you are not likely to date their niece, donate to their cause, contribute to their son's baseball team, introduce them to important people, or park your Bentley in their driveway—they don't really want to know more about you.

A real estate agent, college development officer, and the head of a large local charity may be easy to talk to, but in certain settings their main agenda may be their list of clients, contacts, or supporters—not their pursuit of personal friendships. When this type of networking is the norm, you can still have a lot of fun if you keep your ears open and adjust your expectations.

At a Committee Meeting

One usually gets on better with people when one is making plans than when one is talking about nothing in particular.
—C. S. Lewis, *The Horse and His Boy,* 1954

One of the pleasures of professional work, volunteer work, many artistic efforts, and sports is that you get to know the people on your team and bond with them over a shared goal. Although you strengthen your personal connection with people when you share a project with them, you still need to follow the rules:

Do:

➤ Chat before and after, not during, the meeting.

➤ Turn off your cell phone.

➤ Listen respectfully to what others have to say.

➤ Stick to the agenda.

➤ Disagree courteously. The meeting is not about you; it's about the project.

➤ Offer your expertise when appropriate.

Don't:

- ➤ Ramble on.

- ➤ Interrupt.

- ➤ Carry on private conversations or lobby for support.

- ➤ Let your desire for approval make you mealymouthed and conciliatory when the members of the meeting need to make informed decisions.

- ➤ Allow your wish to be noticed lead you to overcontribute your opinions. Keep your mouth closed when you have nothing to say.

- ➤ Speak reactively, without thinking first.

- ➤ Get personal in your criticism or support.

Jury duty is an odd kind of team. It forces you to work intensely with total strangers to reach a decision that really matters. Although personalities should not enter into the deliberations, your trust in one another is essential to reaching a reasonable verdict. Even here, work you don't choose, with people you don't know, can be eased with civilized conversation.

In a Receiving Line

Deviate from conventional forms of greeting at your peril.
—Thomas E. Hill, *Hill's Manual of Social and Business Forms*, 1873

After weddings, worship services, and speeches, the main participants often welcome guests by "receiving" them. A receiving line is a good way to ensure that each guest is acknowledged, however briefly, because often the bride and groom, clergyperson, or speaker must greet more than a hundred people who are in line to shake hands and say hello.

President Franklin Roosevelt liked to entertain himself in the midst of predictable small talk in White House receiving lines. To see if his guests were really engaged in these mostly superficial exchanges, he sometimes greeted them with "I murdered my grandmother this morning." Often they would reply automatically with "Yes! Wonderful! How nice!" Once a guest who was really paying attention replied politely, "I'm sure she had it coming to her."

You can make the most of a chat in a receiving line and help this traditional but sensible custom work smoothly if you steer between the mechanically polite, meaningless greeting and the overly talkative, needlessly informative exchange.

Do:

➤ Introduce yourself and state your connection to the guest of honor ("I'm Katie and I work in accounting with Scott").

➤ Say "Congratulations!" "Best wishes." "That was a lovely wedding." Old-fashioned manners suggest that you congratulate the groom while you wish the bride well. (For some reason, congratulating the bride might unmask the grim fact that she actually caught him, rather than maintaining the pleasant fiction that *he* caught *her*. Without insulting her taste in men, imply that he's the lucky one.)

➤ If you are the host, thank your guest for coming.

➤ If you are the bride or groom, resist the temptation to thank each guest for a gift. Doing so will slow down the line. If you must say something about a present, don't launch into a verbal thank-you unless you remember exactly what it was. It's better to thank your guest briefly for coming to the shower or wedding instead and send a thank-you note later.

Don't:

➤ Expect the host or anyone else in the receiving line to recall your name immediately. Spare any awkwardness by providing it first.

➤ Engage in extended conversations that will hold up the people who are waiting behind you.

➤ Talk about your own wedding day. Keep the focus off yourself.

At a Shower

Shower the people you love with love.
—James Taylor, "Shower the People," 1976

A shower is a happy prelude to a big event that often includes, but is not only about, the giving of presents. The bigger theme is the pleasure of celebrating a major milestone in life, before the realities actually set in. As a guest, your job is to support this theme, even if you have not experienced this rite of passage—be it a wedding or the birth of a child. As a guest of honor, it is your role to reflect the joy that others are feeling for you without wallowing in it. As a host, it is your task to be sure that all the guests enjoy themselves and connect with one another.

Do:

➤ Make an effort to converse with the family and friends of the bride if you only know the groom, and vice versa. Remember, the newlyweds are still forming a relationship with the other family. Friends who make these connections can extend the network of support across the aisle and help to create a village in which new parents can raise a child.

➤ Keep talk about yourself to a reasonable level, even if you are the bride, mother-to-be, or birthday boy. Real grown-ups share the spotlight.

Don't:

➤ Exclaim "I thought you would never get married!" or "Your lives are never going to be the same [after the baby comes]!"

➤ Talk about the bride or groom's ex-spouse or ex–significant other.

➤ Share embarrassing anecdotes from the guest of honor's childhood or youth.

➤ Tell pregnant women stories about difficult deliveries or sick babies. Don't dramatize your own wedding disaster tales or honeymoon adjustments.

➤ Compare your gift with others, especially with mock humility, fishing for reassurance.

➤ Let a friend's change in status alter your connection to her. If marriage or parenthood is going to change her enough to cool the relationship, don't let the change arise because of conversational gaffes that you have made.

The People You Meet: The Tunnel Visionary

People who are confronted with a turning point or milestone in life can seem to be wearing blinders, and their concerns can hold a normal conversation hostage by directing every tangent of talk back to themselves with phrases like "But getting back to [my situation]" and "As I was saying. . . ."

Watch out for the workaholic: avoid shoptalk unless the social occasion is actually about business. Also, be considerate of people (such as the soon-to-be married, college applicants, new mothers, and the newly bereaved) who are temporarily preoccupied with their own issues. Some of these cares can lead to isolation, and lonely people converse a little differently, even when they're out in public.

Many women find that their reentry to the "real world" after a few days, weeks, or months with a newborn infant is a mind-boggling conceptual leap. I appreciated the friends who would listen to my details about child care for a generous portion of the time, sympathize or praise wholeheartedly, and then lift me out of the baby world with some questions about other facets of my life and some conversation about what they were involved in.

To be supportive, you do need to acknowledge that when someone has reached a milestone, this is her moment. Give her a chance to enjoy sharing the details. Nevertheless, you'll have to meet her more than halfway in conversation and help her relate her situation to what's going on in the outside world. Respect the all-consuming, life-altering experience she is going through while you lead the conversation to a point somewhere between her reality and your everyday life.

In the Hospital

A Muslim has five duties towards another Muslim: to return a salutation, visit the sick, follow funerals, accept an invitation, and say "Allah have mercy on you" when one sneezes.

—Muhammad, from *Sayings of Muhammad,* by Ghazi Ahmad, 1980

Most religions view visits to the sick as acts of virtue. Buddhism prescribes visiting the sick as an act of loving-kindness. Judaism classifies it as a *mitzvah,* or blessing: "Just as God visits the sick, so too should you visit them." Jesus instructed his followers to practice this act of sanctity when he said, "I was sick and ye visited me." Islam decrees that visiting the sick "shows a . . . person that although he is healthy, he . . . is no more entitled to life than the sick person." All of these belief systems suggest that the visitor shares a blessing; he does not bestow it.

In addition to stopping by to see a person in the hospital, you can pay visits to shut-ins and the elderly. Don't avoid such visits because your inner self is whimpering "I won't know what to say." That awkwardness is an integral part of the experience and should not prevent you from doing the right thing. Illness has many aspects of the worst punishment that prison can inflict. It can mean solitary confinement without freedom of movement. A bedridden patient and a shut-in person are hungry for real conversation. They will benefit from human contact, and you will bring something away from the encounter too.

Don't visit if you have the sniffles or if you are in a bad mood. Call ahead to ask about the best time for visiting and whether you can bring something that the ill person needs. Make the offer specific, as in "I'm picking up a few things from the grocery store. Do you want any magazines, tape, toothpaste, or barrettes?" or "I have to run to the post office on the way. Can I get you stamps or pick up your packages?"

You might also tell the sick person or caregiver that you'll be running your own errands soon, and ask him or her to think about it and have a request ready. Too many people like to pretend that they don't need help. If you ask "What do you need? What can I do for you?" without giving them time to think, they will usually say "Oh, nothing, I'm managing just fine." If you focus your question with specifics—"Can I set you up with some music to listen to or some books on tape from the library?"—you may get a yes.

Knock before you enter a sickroom. The sick person has already lost a lot of autonomy. Be sensitive to roommates, and respect everyone's need for privacy.

At the door, ask "Is this a good time to visit?" Hospital patients may look like they have nothing to do all day, but in fact they're prisoners of routine and probably have only a few hours when they are really up to being visited.

You can take another person along if going alone would be too awkward or intense, or tiring for the patient. That way you can make it a three-way conversation. Don't take more than one other person, though—more than two visitors in a hospital room will tire the patient.

Don't sit on the bed if it crowds the person who is ill. Sit in a chair next to the bed, or stand at the foot. Keep eye contact, but also look where the patient is looking from time to time.

Follow the tips in this section if you wish to be a visitor who helps someone feel better by speaking words of comfort. Have one or two topics ready, or bring something to talk about. A gift beyond flowers or candy (an art print, a photo, some music, a book, or a news clipping) can brighten the person's confinement. In conversation with a person who is ill,

Do:

> Ask about his or her condition. Listen courteously.

> Be ready to let your friend express anger. Don't argue back. Say "It is not fair. It must be really difficult to accept. I'd be angry too."

> Say "Tell me about being here," "When is your best time of day?" "What's your day like?" and (if it's even remotely true), "You look better."

> Leave the room if the doctor or a staff person comes in. If you overhear details, don't gossip about them.

> Offer to read aloud. This fills the conversational gap and connects the patient to another world. It is less tiring than holding up his end of the conversation.

Don't:

> Say "You look great" (if it's really not true) or "You look terrible" (even if it is).

> Tell new mothers sad stories if their baby had a rough start—difficult delivery, jaundice, slight abnormalities, hernias, and bruises. These issues will soon recede into the fog of memory, but the parents won't forget that you added to their distress with your gloom and doom.

> Refer to your visit as a duty.

> Compete.

> Catastrophize: "Oh, my God, this is awful." "Oh, how can you stand it?"

> Disparage his surroundings (hospital food, bed, view from the window, or personnel), even if he does.

➤ Chat with sick people about others you know who got worse or didn't make it.

Clergy who visit the sick recommend limiting each visit to ten to fifteen minutes and making a number of short visits rather than one long one. A member of the clergy said, "The best visit is every third day; the best stay is the blink of an eye." One patient commented, "I loved visiting with my friends, but it wasn't until after they left that I realized how much it took out of me." Watch for signs that you have stayed long enough.

Staying the Course

In the end, there is no desire so deep as the desire for companionship.
—Graham Greene, 1904–1991

Once in a while you will have the opportunity to talk with a friend who is so ill that she does not expect to live. Many people, when faced with this situation, make excuses not to visit: "She doesn't want to see me." "I don't know what to say." "I'm too upset." You will probably have to override your instinctive reluctance and follow the wisdom of Immanuel Kant: "I ought, therefore I can."

Rely on the experts; when in doubt, make the visit. Lindsay McGrath, a hospital chaplain, advises, "Woody Allen said it best—'Ninety percent of life is just showing up.' Even though it's been my job for a long time to visit very ill people, I find that just showing up is never easy. But it's *always* worthwhile." Remind yourself that when a friend dies without warning, your enduring regret is always "Oh, I wish I'd had a chance to say good-bye." Take that chance. It's the right thing, not the easy thing, to do.

Speak with your friend's caregiver or nurse ahead of time to ensure that you're making your visit at the most convenient time.

Another hospital chaplain, Leonie Luterman, advises that when you arrive at the hospital, allow yourself a warming up period of five to ten minutes in your car or in the coffee shop to collect your thoughts (and do the same when you leave, to let yourself decompress).

When you get close to the hospital room, stop by the nurses' station to see how your friend and her family are doing. Family members are hurting too, and often they don't get the attention they need.

Prepare yourself for the distress of seeing pain that won't go away, unhappiness that has no solution, and illness that can't be cured by anything you can do or say. Have faith that these forms of suffering can be eased through conversation.

Touch the person if it is not physically uncomfortable for her. Hold hands, smile, and listen patiently. Follow her lead. Ask her where she would like you to sit. At first, say something:

➤ How are you doing today?

➤ I'm here. I care about you.

➤ This seems hard. How are you holding up?

➤ I don't really know what to say.

➤ I want to tell you that you mean so much to me.

Ask her what she would like to do or talk about. Listen. Sometimes people are eager to talk about their impending death or worsening condition directly; others want to talk about anything but that.

Offer conversational openers that address the whole person, not just the illness. Beneath the day-to-day difficulty and pain, a dying person is struggling to maintain a core of identity. As a hospice patient put it, "When I talk with my friends, I am 'me' again."

Encourage your friend to talk about what's left, not what has been lost.

Follow the ten rules of conversation: especially, don't ramble. Be present and open. Be sensitive to the fact that your life is the same; she is the one who is making the journey. Also, don't:

➤ Comment on her appearance or the paraphernalia of terminal illness (oxygen tent, morphine pump).

➤ Pretend that everything is going to turn out okay when it's clearly not.

➤ Argue.

➤ Try to "fix" her situation.

➤ Decline to talk about what she wants to talk about or hush her if she wants to talk about death.

➤ Comment about your own distress at seeing her diminished. She is already at a disadvantage in being bedridden, wearing a hospital gown, feeling disabled, needing help, and wanting more time. It's not about you. Show her that she is still the person you know and care about.

Be attuned to signs that your friend wants to deal with unfinished business and needs help—either practical help with business matters or emotional help with unresolved feelings. She needs to feel that her life and this part of it have been meaningful and worthwhile and that she is loved.

If the dying person is not able to speak, talk to her anyway. Honor the person she was by continuing to connect with the person she has become. If she is comatose, act on the assumption that she is still there. Even if the conversation is one-way, your relationship still exists—she is still eliciting something from you. Keep that relationship alive by looking past appearances and speaking to the person. Read to her, talk about current events, and recall long-ago memories.

Stay alert for cues that your visit has lasted long enough, and, if she can speak, ask her if she would like you to come again. Thank her for letting you spend time with her.

Visiting the sick is a privilege, an act of loving-kindness, not a duty. Although there are no dress rehearsals for death, by joining your friend for a few steps in her journey, you may be more at peace with your own mortality. She may offer you a glimpse of an experience that you will someday share.

At a Wake or Funeral, and Afterward

I felt it shelter to speak to you.
—Emily Dickinson, from a letter, 1878

Whether you are visiting someone in a hospital or talking with someone who has lost a loved one, conversation is at its most civilized when it comforts people. Sometimes words are the only thing that can. What you say to someone in grief makes a tremendous difference to his feelings both before and after a death.

Unfortunately, the impulse to speak words of comfort doesn't always translate into just the right phrase. In grief, as in other times of stress, emotions are raw and wounds are easy to inflict. Talking with a bereaved person can be difficult and uncomfortable. When you attend a funeral or a wake, go to a memorial service later on, or encounter a grieving person for at least a year afterward, you will need to take special care not only to say words of comfort but also to avoid words that hurt.

You may be uncertain of which words are expected and which words are taboo. Although, as essayist C. S. Lewis said, "None of us grieves in a straight line," most people express sorrow the way their culture or religion has taught them. If you're not Irish, you may be confused by the high spirits at a wake, where people vent both their celebration of a life with exuberant toasts and their sadness with sobs, wailing, and keening. If you're not Jewish, you will have to learn about sitting shiva and the mourning ritual that takes days to conclude. If you come from outside the Yankee tradition, you may mistake a stiff upper lip for an absence of sorrow.

It's always important to respect the religious and cultural customs of the bereaved family, and learning about how people all over the world put their grief into words may give you special insight when you choose what to say. In Java, for instance, a deeply bereft young husband makes the effort to smile and greet everyone kindly. He describes this evenness of voice as his way to flatten out the hills and valleys of his internal emotional plain. In Africa, in the Dagura culture, people set aside a designated space at the memorial gathering where emotional outbursts are "contained." Outside this space, mourners must not cry, dance, or speak about how they are feeling. Special helpers guide people back in if they have strayed out of the ritual space where it is safe to let their grief out. Even in America, mourning at a Greek funeral is considered the job of the women; their demonstrative, ritualized weeping and despair act out the grief that the men must repress.

There are many ways to understand someone's grief and to comfort the pain behind it. Use tact and sensitivity around the bereaved. Once you have been through the death of a parent, spouse, or child, you will know how to start the conversation, but until then, feel your way with phrases that keep you out of the spotlight and dim its glare for the person who is mourning. Don't fill in the conversation with extraneous outside news or push your religious beliefs, use clichés, or talk about your own losses and problems. Never complain about your own loved ones while you're trying to comfort people who have lost theirs.

When you attend a wake, funeral, or memorial service, speak on behalf of your family members who could not attend: "Fred and I are so sorry." "My mom said to tell you she wishes she could have been here." Don't overexplain. For instance, it's cruel to tell a new widow that your own husband had to be at an important business meeting.

Use the deceased's name, especially for a baby. Never blame a lung cancer victim for smoking, a teenager for risky behavior.

Find a way to acknowledge the bereaved person's sadness while adding something positive: "In all this, I can see that your daughter is a real comfort."

If it seems appropriate to do so, share a fond or funny memory of the deceased. Pass along anything the person said that reflected kindly on his or her loved ones. Too much sorrow and solemnity can be out of place at most gatherings (although some are very grim). By focusing on your own sad memories, you take the attention away from those who are closer to the family.

At the funeral, don't say, when faced with an open casket, that the person "looks good." Comment instead on what a handsome man he was or on a special tie or ring that he is wearing. In fact, it's most appropriate to approach the casket alone and make no comment at all.

In a receiving line at a funeral or memorial service, if someone says "Thank you for coming," don't reply "I wouldn't have missed it for the world." Just as with any other receiving line, keep your remarks kind and brief. Don't expect the bereaved to spend much if any time with you. Don't monopolize them.

Here are some words to use when you speak to anyone who has lost a loved one:

Express your concern for the person who is grieving:

➤ I'm sorry./I'm sad for you.

➤ We're thinking of you./We wish we could comfort you.

➤ How are you doing with all this?

➤ I'm here and I want to listen.

➤ Please tell me what you are feeling./I'd like to spend time talking with you when you're ready.

➤ It isn't fair, is it?/This must be hard for you./What's the hardest part for you?

➤ Take all the time you need.

Don't say anything that trivializes the person's grief:

➤ It's better this way./At least she is not suffering.

➤ Stay busy and get your mind off your troubles./Life must go on./You can put it behind you./You should get on with your life.

➤ You'll recover. (Bereavement is like an amputation, not an illness. A person who is grieving is not ill, and grief does not go away like the flu.)

➤ Anything that begins "You should."

➤ You're so strong. (Bereaved people feel numb and fragile.)

Don't say anything that turns the focus on yourself:

➤ Why didn't you call me?

➤ I know just how you feel.

➤ It's awful. I'm so upset over this. I'm heartbroken.

➤ The same thing happened to me, only worse.

➤ No one will miss him more than me.

Do express your appreciation of the person who has died:

➤ We all miss him so much./I have such good memories of him./I will always remember him.

➤ He had a wonderful life.

➤ He had so many people who loved him.

➤ It was so nice knowing he was there./He was such a great neighbor/colleague/coach/supporter . . . (rather than just "He was a wonderful person").

➤ We always enjoyed her sense of humor.

Don't say anything that diminishes the importance of the person who has died:

➤ How old was he? (as if you'd miss an older person less)

➤ I didn't really know him.

➤ He would have wanted . . .

To a religious person, you may say:

➤ You are in our prayers.

➤ We know God is with you in this.

Don't say:

➣ God doesn't give you more than you can handle.

To someone who has lost a loved one after an accident or suicide, say:

➣ I don't know why it happened.
➣ This was such a shock.

Don't say:

➣ Didn't you notice something was wrong?
➣ How did he do it? Did he leave a note?
➣ He was always a little unstable.

To someone who has lost a child, say:

➣ To have a new life end so suddenly is sad.
➣ He was such a great kid. He had a lot of potential.

Don't say:

➣ You can always have another baby./You can always have more children./You can always adopt.
➣ It's good you have other children./It's too bad you don't have other children.
➣ It's probably a blessing.
➣ You didn't have time to get attached.

To someone who has lost a spouse, don't say:

➣ You look great. You won't have any trouble finding someone new.
➣ Will you date again?

If you want to offer practical help, say:

➤ I'll call you next week (and do it!)

Don't say:

➤ Call me if you need anything. (People who are grieving may not be able to figure out what they need or how to ask for it.)

Finally, don't be the last person to leave a wake or funeral. Don't linger with close family unless you are sure you are needed.

After the Grieving Rituals Are Over

In *A Grief Observed* (1961), C. S. Lewis wrote about the discomfort that he experienced in social situations shortly after the death of his wife:

> *An odd by-product of my loss is that I'm aware of being an embarrassment to everyone I meet. At work, at the club, in the street, I see people, as they approach me, trying to make up their minds whether they'll say something about it or not. I hate it if they do, and if they don't. . . . I like best the well brought-up young men . . . who walk up to me as if I were a dentist, turn very red, get it over, and then edge away to the bar as quickly as they decently can.*

A person who has experienced a loss can feel like a leper if people avoid talking with him. This form of social isolation is an additional burden on top of his grief. People often don't say anything out of fear of saying the wrong thing. When in doubt, offer at least a few words. You can leave room in the conversation for the other person to continue with the subject or not if he wishes, but at least take the first step of saying something.

Continue to stay connected to a person who is grieving long after the funeral is over. Contact the person who is grieving often, and let him talk about details if he wishes. Listen.

If you missed the wake or funeral for any reason, apologize. Don't confess to the grieving person, "I didn't call you or attend the wake because I didn't know what to say."

Offer to help in concrete ways:

> I'll bring dinner over on Tuesday. Would that be convenient for you?

> If I could help [by finding a source of assistance, such as a house cleaner or someone to do yard work; doing a chore; coming over; listening], please let me know.

Express your condolence for several weeks and whenever you encounter the bereaved person. After that, ask him how he is doing, with special reference to his loved one. Ask after the greater group of bereaved: "How is your sister taking this?" And remember to mention his loved one on her birthday, their anniversary, at holidays, and a year after the funeral.

Conversation with a Grieving Child

We should not make light of the troubles of children. They are worse than ours, because we can see the end of our troubles and they can never see any end.

—William Middleton, as quoted by his nephew,
  W. B. Yeats, *Autobiographies,* 1935

Children who have lost a loved one grieve as much as adults do—maybe more—but they show it in different ways. Often they experience emotions that they can't verbalize, and their reactions may not resemble the grief reactions of adults. They may

What to Say about Miscarriage

A close family friend knew I was pregnant, and no one told her that I'd miscarried. She saw me across the room (my head only) and shouted, "Hey! Let me see how big you are!" The room fell silent, and I said that I had lost the baby and promptly broke down in tears. She took me in the next room and told me she was sorry it happened and proceeded to validate that I had been pregnant, it was real, and it was a real loss. After our talk I felt so much better.

—Anonymous

One of the hardest deaths to find words of comfort for is a miscarriage. Miscarriage thwarts the parents' most primal instinct, to protect their child. What seemed like a process deep inside the safety of the mother's own body is revealed as something completely beyond her control. Women may feel profound guilt that something they did or didn't do was responsible. The future envisioned for this person-to-be has been destroyed without even the consolation that a funeral would bring.

American society has no rituals to acknowledge the sorrow of miscarriage, and so the sufferers cannot formally acknowledge their loss. For all of these reasons, couples who have experienced a miscarriage may be especially vulnerable when other people respond to their grief with silence or when they make well-intentioned but often off-the-mark and hurtful comments.

One woman who has had more than one miscarriage said it best: "The support that helped most was from friends who understood that this is *a death in the family*—and treated it that way." (While most sympathy goes to the mother because she is more physically affected, the father hurts in his own way.) The obvious truth like "You can try again" or "Many pregnancies end in miscarriage" is just too hard for the parents to hear. On the other hand, saying nothing implies that the loss doesn't matter. If someone you know has experienced a miscarriage, make sure she knows that you sympathize and recognize that she is going through a terrible time. Acknowledge that she has experienced a real loss of a real child.

Simply say "I'm so sorry." Then take your cues from her. Offer to listen if she needs to talk about it.

When asked about conversations that comforted her, one woman said, "What I wanted most from friends was to cry and be silent and for us both to be comfortable in that silence." Other sufferers have said they were comforted by calls and cards and by people who kept in touch and followed up a week or two later. Call and ask to drop off food, flowers, or a book, and make it clear that you are ready to come in only if your friend feels like company.

Don't ignore the situation or pretend that nothing has happened or say nothing out of fear of saying the wrong thing. Also, just as with any death, avoid heartless comments like "It's the way nature corrects her errors." Don't call the baby "the fetus," "the pregnancy," or "it." Never say "Just move on" or suggest that she will "get over it." Many mothers recall the anniversary of the lost child's due date for years to come. Don't talk about "next time."

smile and go off to play when you break the news that someone has died. Others will be sad and physical: they will yell, bicker with each other, and be aggressive with those around them and with objects. Children sometimes express grief by yelling, pounding, or running it out. Never assume that a child who is not crying is not hurting; some children who are grieving cry and some don't.

You can be of comfort and help when you talk with them if you keep these guidelines in mind. First of all, grief therapists say that "if it's unmentionable, it's unmanageable." Acknowledge their loss and answer their questions without the use of euphemisms (say "Betty died," not "Betty left" or "We lost Betty"). Expressions like "She's gone" or "He passed away" can confuse a child and evoke an unfocused sense of guilt. Gently and clearly say what happened, without sweetening it beyond recognition. Especially with young children, hazy terms for death like "He went to sleep" will not help them deal with reality.

Listen to children who are grieving. Parents, therapists, counselors, and friends should be with children to help them, not "fix them" or "help them get over it," or "move beyond it." Include children in funerals and memorial services in order to give them an opportunity to say good-bye and to grieve.

Don't pretend nothing is wrong or that a child's grief is not as important as an adult's. Don't be afraid to show your feelings. Sometimes adults are reluctant to cry in front of a child, but tears give her permission to express her sorrow too. Don't show violent emotion, but do be honest: "I really miss Grandma. I'm crying because I miss her."

Children are sensitive to the emotions of those around them, even though they are sometimes unable to give voice to their own.

Furthermore, a child's grief may be eclipsed by the greater and more articulated grief of others. When a child loses a parent, a sibling, or a grandparent, the survivors may simply not have the strength to comfort themselves *and* the mourning child. It's important to grieve together.

Our culture gives children mixed messages about death. Halloween is a gleeful, childish holiday based on death symbols. Violent death is realistically and sometimes flippantly simulated in movies. These portrayals of death rarely allude to the grief that follows.

In contrast to these two extreme images, real death is hidden away; no wonder it is scary and incomprehensible! Dramatists from the early Greeks on have known that if death and violence take place offstage, what the viewer will imagine is more frightening than any reality. Take the terror out of death by answering the child's questions frankly.

Children may be confused as well as sad. Don't put on too brave a face or try to find something good to say like "Aren't you glad Mommy doesn't hurt anymore?" or "Isn't it wonderful that God's love was shared at the funeral?"

Let the child initiate and steer the conversation, and provide healthy outlets like a punching bag or an afternoon of throwing rocks into the ocean. Talk about the loss whenever he brings up the subject, and answer only the questions that he asks—don't overwhelm him with information. Let him control what he is ready to hear. Children can handle only segments of grief at a time. He may not always want to talk about death.

When you have a conversation with a child about death, touch, hold, or hug her, but always with her permission.

Do:

➤ Answer her questions honestly.

➤ Share a memory of her loved one.

➤ Reassure her that she did not cause the death by her angry thoughts or insignificant mistakes. Try to find out what she thinks happened by asking her to tell you.

➤ Be helpful but not all-knowing. "I don't know" is a good answer to "why" questions.

➤ Tell the truth about the possibility of the child's death or your own. Don't promise that you won't die. You can say "I think I will live until I am very, very old, but no one knows for sure."

Do say:

➤ The person's name, for example: "I know your Grandpa died, and I'm sure you miss him very much."

➤ Nobody knows for sure, but I believe that her spirit is somewhere happy.

➤ It's nobody's fault when somebody dies.

➤ The exact cause of death: "Grandma's heart wouldn't work anymore."

➤ I know you will miss her.

➤ It's okay to be sad./It's okay to be angry.

Don't say:

➤ Now you have to be a big boy.

➤ Don't cry.

From the most casual encounters on the street or in an elevator to the most intense exchanges surrounding the death of a loved one, life offers continual opportunities for us to reach out to other people with words. If you consider some of this chapter's civilized expressions, you will be equipped to convey something more meaningful when you speak—you will be able to transform situations into real conversations.

· VI ·

Conversations with Younger and Older People

*One of the greatest pleasures of life is conversation (and I
particularly like men, women, and children).*

—The Reverend Sydney Smith, 1877

M<small>ANY ROUTINES</small> of life channel you into conversations with people who share your age, your
occupation, your income, your politics, or your
neighborhood. Of course it's easy to talk with them; you already
have so many experiences in common. This cozy exchange of similar ideas may be comfortable, but the tendency to talk only with
like-minded individuals can lead to a closed loop that won't challenge your thoughts or sharpen your social skills.

When I was a college student, I used to take off-campus baby-
sitting jobs not just for the pocket money, but to get into a world
where everyone was not between the ages of eighteen and twenty-
two. I needed the fresh perspective that I could get from a toddler's fantasy about a Play-Doh creation or a fifth grader's
melodramatic tale of playground loyalties and betrayals. My ability to talk to anyone outside my narrow age bracket felt like a mus-
cle I needed to flex to help me keep my balance.

If you have read chapter V, you know how to make the most of
conversations wherever they offer themselves. Speaking up in a

new situation will lead you to widen your circle of friends and meet people who are different, sometimes very different, from you. In addition to talking with people outside your usual routine, you can enrich your life by talking with people who are older or younger than you. Reaching beyond your own generation will open your eyes to a broader landscape of human experience. This chapter will provide you with tools to recognize the way that people speak at different stages of their lives. If you use these tools to open up some conversations, you'll soon be welcomed, entertained, and inspired by people of any age.

How to Talk with Children

A person's a person, no matter how small.
—Dr. Seuss, *Horton Hears a Who,* 1954

Simple differences in language development can hinder conversation between you and someone who is much younger unless you bridge that gap. You can adapt your approach to every child, regardless of whether he is a baby, preschooler, child, or teenager.

How to Talk with Babies

Babies have different temperaments that become apparent as they spend time with you. Some babies are quiet when they first meet an unfamiliar person; others gurgle with excitement, make eye contact, and squirm to let you know they want to interact. Pay attention to a baby's first reactions to your presence.

If a baby is in her mother's or father's arms, say her name, offer her a toy or key ring, and let her see that her parent approves of you before you expect her to warm up to you. If she withdraws toward her mother or seems overwhelmed and freezes, step back and just smile at her. Some babies experience stranger anxiety, so be respectful if she does not want to go to you. She may feel most comfortable if you move carefully and talk very softly.

If she extends her hands and smiles at you, reach for her and ask her mother if you can hold her. If she agrees, gently pick the baby up and cradle her in your arms. Watch her face at all times. Let her keep her mother in her field of vision. Don't be surprised if she wants to be returned to her mother right away.

When you talk to a young baby who is in a crib or on the floor, use a gentle, neutral tone of voice and move slowly into her view or play space. Listen to her sounds and imitate them. As you do so, vary your voice pattern. Smile and make eye contact. Follow a simple rule of thumb in responding to a baby's babble: mimic the sounds made by a baby under a year old. Translate into correct pronunciation the sounds made by a baby over twelve months old. For example, if a ten-month-old baby says, "Podee? Podee?" imitate her: "Podee! Podee!" If a two-year-old toddler says, "Iddle podee?" give her the real words: "Little pony, yes!" And extend the conversation: "Little blue pony."

How to Talk with Preschoolers

Before one went to school, almost every new human
being one met seemed a stimulant; that is to say,
if they took any notice of the small.
—Maurice Baring, *Lost Lectures*, 1971

From ages one to five, little children vary in their reactions to new people and places. Most toddlers love to explore and discover new things. By the time a child is about seventeen months, he is willing to leave his parent and play with others. Some children are more sensitive than others to a parent's departure from a room, but others have no fear about spending time with an unfamiliar person.

When you approach a toddler, watch him to see if he stops playing and becomes quiet. Some children will immediately begin to play with you, while others will stay near their parent or remain quiet until they feel safe. Move slowly into the toddler's play space and begin to play with a similar toy. As you talk:

Do:

➤ Describe both your actions and his actions in play. Say things like: "Oh, look at this plane! It's going to the airport. Here I go! I'm a pilot! We're flying."

➤ Vary your voice patterns in a playful way.

➤ Listen to what he says, and follow his lead.

➤ Use facial expressions and gestures as well as words.

Don't:

➤ Try to cajole a small child into speaking to you if he has never met you before. It flatters your vanity, but it confuses the child, who has probably been taught "never speak to strangers," and it leaves him vulnerable in the future to trusting some stranger he shouldn't.

➤ Take offense if he seems to tune you out when he plays.

➤ Talk constantly.

➤ Argue with him or try to discipline him.

➤ Talk baby talk long after he's moved on to real talk.

Some toddlers may respond on autopilot to the routine conversation openers ("What's your name?" "How old are you?").

One of my toddlers learned quickly what to expect, so that after providing his name when people asked, he always held up three fingers before they even asked the inevitable next question about his age. Even toddlers who have experience with these questions may not know how to take the conversation any further. You'll have more luck really talking with him if, instead of asking closed, vague, formulaic questions like "How old are you?" you talk about what is going on around him or what he is doing, using open, specific, and simple questions: "How do you play that game?" "How did you make the snowman's feet?"

Toddlers, like people of all ages, are sensitive to being patronized. Don't talk down to them, refer to them in the third person, or trivialize them. If you announce to everyone "What a big boy he is. Look at him!" he'll be embarrassed and confused. To begin a conversation "Oh, aren't you a cute little thing" does not work as well as "I like your red kitty. What's his name?"

How to Talk with School-Age Children

To talk to a child, to fascinate him, is much more difficult than to win an electoral victory. But it is also more rewarding.
—Colette, *Journey for Myself,* 1971

When you talk with a child, get her name right. Don't invent or dredge up infantile nicknames, or presume that you are entitled to use the diminutives her family uses.

Also, be concrete. Most school-age children prefer to talk about specific things and events rather than abstract ideas. It never hurts, when visiting, to bring them a special book or game to talk about. Ask open-ended questions like "Do you have pets?"

Ask about subjects that preoccupy children every day—their room, their friends, their lunch, their games, and their homework topics. For example, you might ask: "Do you have science in school? What are you studying? Weather or geology?" Then you can engage them in a real conversation by asking very specific questions, such as "You're studying climate in science? Have you gotten to the names of clouds yet?" Ask about their hobbies and interests, like dinosaurs, kinds of medieval armor, animal care, food, cars, and sports—something large and many-sided that will let them tell you what they know (and maybe you don't) at their own level.

Ask specific questions, but don't be an interrogator. If you know each other well, you can ask, "What were the best and worst things that happened today (or this week, or over the vacation)?"

Be courteous. To teach kids courtesy in conversation, be polite yourself; stay at their level, and don't trump every statement with some superior knowledge of your own. I once watched a filmed conversation between atomic physicist Edward Teller, then in his eighties, and a twelve-year-old whiz kid who had recently won a science prize. Teller lured the boy out of his depth into a discussion of Mideast politics, something even adults find difficult to understand, instead of just asking him about his science project and letting him shine at his own level.

In order to keep the respect flowing both ways, watch what you say. A child may be frighteningly candid as he boomerangs your own lack of manners right back at you. For instance, if you say "You're a lot taller than I remember you" (did you really expect a child to get smaller?), don't be surprised if he replies "You're a lot grayer than I remember *you.*" Or "Here's my little sweetie. Have you been avoiding me?" "Yes, your breath is always stinky."

Whether they deliver zingers out of a spirit of experiment, bald honesty, or in response to your own blunders, elementary-school-age children may say things that are inappropriate. When they do, ignore the comment and divert them to another topic. In response to gems like "You're so old! You're older than my grandfather, and he's dead," you can smile and laugh and say "That's what happens to everyone. But, guess what? I get more candles on my birthday cake!" Hang on to your sense of humor, but don't indulge it at a child's expense.

Watch out for young children trying out their potty mouths on you to see if they can get away with it. Don't overreact or sound shocked. Ask pleasantly "Do you know what that means?" They almost never do, and are abashed when you tell them that it's something to save for the bathroom or bedroom.

Older school-age children sometimes use words that offend others. They may insult someone you know, or even you. The best way to respond is to be direct. Use "I" messages, such as "I feel disappointed when you tell me things like that." Or "I know that may be true, but I don't want to hear mean things about other people. I think that's being critical." "I'm not used to the f word, so can you find another way to say that?"

You can't prevent children from hearing some !@#$%^&*+? expressions in the course of the week, but you don't have to give those words the stamp of adult approval by using them yourself. Speak with care. You're in the driver's seat; you can steer the conversation away from the gutter.

Just as you keep children's spicy language in perspective, accept their compliments in the spirit in which they are given. If a six-year-old says "I liked the socks you gave me, but I hated the sweater," just chuckle and say "Then I'll have to give you more socks next time and find someone you can give that sweater to." If she asks you why you are so wrinkled, you might explain: "I've got one wrinkle for each year." Don't act shocked and tell her what a naughty little girl she is. Her parents probably told her that she should tell the truth.

Sometimes it's tempting to talk about adult topics over the heads of children. Don't. Adults may think they can fool children by using code words or spelling out key topics. They forget that children are absolute geniuses at penetrating a disguise; a toddler who is years away from reading can pick up that his parents are getting a d-i-v-o-r-c-e. Small children can hear and understand vastly more than they can articulate, and older children have enough of their own issues to attend to without having to hear about yours. All kids are liable to blurt out private secrets to the wrong people. Say "Mandy, Carol and I want to have some private grown-up talk. Could you play here while we go into the kitchen?"

Children really do listen, often at the worst spot in your conversation. Consider the four-year-old who learned etiquette by listening to his parents greet their friends for parties and dinners in their home. When he was introduced to the family's minister after church, his mother prompted him: "What do you say, Jimmy?" and Jimmy replied, "Can I get you a drink?" Children deserve a firewall between themselves and the adult complexities whose catchphrases they so easily absorb—and repeat—without understanding them.

Phrases to avoid when you talk with children:

➤ Which one are you?

➤ You kids . . .

➤ You've grown!

➤ When I was your age . . . (if it sounds condescending)

- ➤ You look just like your father! (can be especially devastating to a girl)/You look just like your mother! (can be mortifying to both mother and daughter)
- ➤ How are your grades?
- ➤ Look at me when I'm talking to you.
- ➤ What are you going to be when you grow up?
- ➤ Are you shy? / What's the matter? Cat got your tongue?

How to Talk with Teenagers and Young Adults

Try to remember the kind of September
When you were a tender and callow fellow.
—Tom Jones, "Try to Remember," 1959

Adults don't have to treat teenagers like aliens. They are not a new plague on the human race that heralds the downfall of civilization. They are simply part adult, part child, in a shifting mixture that has them on a different wavelength every time you encounter them. If the teenager you are with at the moment does talk like an alien, treat this encounter as a chance to enlist an interpreter, not a chance to squelch a Martian.

Teenagers want adults to believe that they are basically intelligent, trustworthy young adults who care about the world. That said, teenagers *do* have their own culture of language, music, and clothing. Their speech seems loud, their vocabulary cryptic, their body language chaotic, and their manners sketchy. Sometimes your first reaction is to mourn the memory of that enchanting toddler and inquisitive child. However, if you show polite interest in the person before you at this moment and the goodwill to search for something to talk about, you can find out who he or she is becoming.

When you talk to any adolescent, the guidelines for civilized conversation among adults usually apply. Greet them with the courtesy you use with adults. Call them what they like to be called. Many children shed even common nicknames when they reach adolescence. Don't be the last to find out that Bobby is now Robert, that Pigface is now Patricia, and that Junior wants to be Carl. They may even want to take a completely different name. Keep checking as they grow up, and respect their identity.

Ask them what they and their friends are most excited about in the worlds of sports, fashion, music, movies, books, magazines, games, schools, and personalities. Explore the exquisite definitions of their various subcultures; your own existence will seem simple after you try to distinguish between them. Looking back on early adolescence, a nineteen-year-old says, "We're easy to flatter; just show a willingness to sample our culture. We'll communicate if we feel you are genuinely interested."

What to say to teenagers:

➣ How do you get to school? What's your commute like?

➣ Are you working this summer?

➣ Is your French class going to Montreal this year?

➣ What group are you listening to most these days?

➣ Have you been to any concerts lately?/Have you seen any good movies recently?

Pay teenagers the compliment of listening to them and reacting genuinely and courteously to what they say. Don't try to catch them out on contradictions, such as "Well, but last year you were a vegetarian . . ." or "You told me that kids who got tattoos are losers. What happened?" Many teenagers don't like criticism (who does?), but they do like to challenge their listeners and often say things to provoke an adult into a reaction; let them see how adults handle disagreement. Adolescence is a time of moodiness and insecurity; model for them how not to overreact.

Respect their need for intellectual privacy. Don't be too nosy; let them decide if you "need to know" their anxieties and failures, or even their dreams and fantasies. Be careful about leading off with "Do you have a boyfriend?" Don't press high school seniors about specific college applications until they know which schools they got into; you wouldn't like to give every busybody a list of the places you applied for a job and got turned down.

Don't force conversation. Any sane person will clam up and start looking for the exit when you say "Let's have a good talk." Likewise, don't talk about how things were and especially about how you were when you were a teenager.

The cute capers of their childhood seem like yesterday to you but ancient history to them. It's rude and hostile and controlling to dwell on it; if you conjure up that little kid, you destroy the fragile and laboriously maintained new adult in front of you. A friend says her teenage daughters won't let her invite over a certain old friend who knew them when they were little, because he just can't let the past go. He tells them over and over, "I remember when you threw up on the merry-go-round ride" or announces to the group, "When I opened the door, Nicki burst out of the door stark naked and ran up and down the sidewalk." She says they not only loathe him but fear him, this well-meaning guy, because it seems to them he uses these little memories to put them down. They wonder what new ammunition he might be gathering to shoot them down in their twenties with the blunders they made in their teens! Teenagers hate to be reminded of things they once did—even good things.

How to Talk with Grown-ups

When I was a boy of fourteen, my father was so ignorant that I could hardly stand to have the old man around. But when I got to be twenty-one, I was astonished at how much he had learned in seven years.
—Often attributed to Mark Twain, 1835–1910

Unless you are the world's oldest human being, you probably have older adults in your life with whom you would like to have good conversations. This section will show you how—whether you are a teenager who must talk with your parents' friends at a Christmas party or you are being checked out by your date's dad. Many adults will be important to you soon, for job hunting, role models, advice, and friendship. A few might even turn out to be your future in-laws.

How to Talk with Adults (if You Are a Teenager)

If you are a teenager talking to adults, bear in mind that while they may have known you as a baby or child, you have grown a lot since then. Grown-ups may not realize that you are not still wearing earphones all the time and have a lot more interesting things to say than "Are we there yet?" Help adults remember who you are while you update them about what you are interested in. Look for something mutually interesting you can talk about. Even if they don't seem to catch on that you've changed a great deal since the last time you met, let them get to know the new improved you. And cut them some slack; they may have teenagers of their own and be unable to communicate well with them right now.

Adults are hugely flattered when teenagers spend time talking with them. It makes them feel as though their youth has not completely passed by. And it broadens their pool of knowledge. You may be able to open a window for them with your ideas. Being able to quote you later, to other adults, will give them an insider's viewpoint and ally them with you and your friends. You'll also earn extra points when you engage in civilized conversation with the parents of your friends.

Look for grown-up-friendly situations to practice talking with them. They're almost human; they like to talk. Try sitting after a meal is over; that's when they like to chat. Also try car rides (when adults often can give you nearly full attention without acknowledging it and talk is welcome), community projects, school events (why be seen talking just to your own parents while other adults are around to practice on?), and parties in your house (your parents will be busy and you will earn brownie points from both sides for help with hosting).

It's easy to get a conversation started with a grown-up:

➤ Take out your gum and take off your earphones.

➤ Don't phrase your statements as questions? You know what I mean? Eliminate the word "like" from your vocabulary.

➤ Smile a little and make eye contact.

➤ Shake hands and greet them by name. They may touch and hug you more than you want right now; but getting your hand out in front of you immediately for them to shake will fend off a lot of that. You can also side-hug them if it makes you more comfortable.

Determine if they themselves are parents. If they have babies, ask politely about them, the same way you would if they had pets.

Don't let them pigeonhole you as a baby-sitter type unless you really need the work. (A good excuse is "I've got too much homework.") If they have little kids, you can ask about what they are doing, and add some interesting stories from your youth.

Listen carefully for clues to what they like to talk about. You probably won't know anything about patent law, economic policy, musicology, neurophysiology, investment banking, or the price of rice futures, but you do know how to listen. If you feel phony pretending to be interested, you can always say "How do you get into that kind of job?" or "I don't know anything about that field."

Deflect any clueless grown-up comments:

➤ If they persist with stories of the younger you, try "I used to do that, but I'm older now."

➤ If they bad-mouth your whole generation because of some imagined activity, don't get mad but say "I haven't gotten into that" or "That's not my thing" or "That sounds amazing! But it doesn't work for me."

➤ If they suggest that your fearless statement of individuality is in fact just what everyone else your age is wearing, you can say with a smile, "I guess it gets us ready to wear suits."

How to Talk with Your In-Laws

The awe and dread with which the untutored savage contemplates his mother-in-law are amongst the most familiar facts of anthropology.
—Sir James George Frazer, *The Golden Bough*, 1922

Learning to talk to your child's friends or your friend's parents is a piece of cake compared with learning to talk to them when they become your in-laws. What you say can help or hurt the relationship, bring you closer or cut you off, take you along interesting avenues, or drag you down the same dead ends.

In-law conversations are complex, too, because of all the bad publicity they've had for centuries. If you are someone's mother-in-law or father-in-law, you may inspire awe, dread, and a host of other emotions. Be ever conscious of your power to hurt and offend and to add stress.

Your child's marriage license does not give you license to say whatever is on your mind. One rule of thumb for good conversations with these transplanted family members is to pretend that you are talking with new acquaintances whom you'd like to befriend, and follow the rules of conversation: don't talk about sensitive subjects, ask questions and listen to the answers, and so on. Size up their tolerance for honesty, advice, and disagreement *before* you open your mouth and announce "I'm still friends with Bob's ex-wife" or "That's not the way to make an omelet." Don't discuss sex, religion, money, child rearing, or politics until you all know one another better.

While taking great care to avoid pitfalls, you also can take steps to make your conversations upbeat and affirming.

Do:

➢ Establish tactfully what you'd like to be called. Don't insist on being everyone's "Mom" if your son-in-law wants to keep that name for his own mother.

➢ Pay attention to the family communication style of your child's spouse—and respect it. If you are more argumentative than your in-law, tone it down. If you are less forthright, learn to interpret what seems like opposition as just openness.

➤ Ask about your children's and grandchildren's activities and learn the names of their friends.

Don't:

➤ Say or imply that your son-in-law or daughter-in-law "isn't really part of the family" in times of crisis. Those words can wound.

➤ Make thoughtless statements about your own child in front of his or her partner: "He's a workaholic just like his father." "She has that Jackson nose."

➤ Criticize his or her choice of baby names.

➤ Criticize or discipline your grandchildren in front of their parents or offer unsolicited parenting expertise.

➤ Use guilt as a weapon. Healthy conversations do not include asking family members to visit because your "days are numbered" (especially if this is not true) or asking them not to take a vacation because something bad might happen to you in their absence.

➤ Ever cut off communication with your in-laws.

➤ Lose your sense of humor.

How to Talk with the Parents of Your Significant Other

Advice columnists will never run out of fodder for their columns as long as there are mothers-in-law in the world. It takes a while to pick up on your new family's own special way of talking. Some misunderstandings are inevitable. Everyone has to get used to parents-in-law. Eleanor Roosevelt's advice that "no one can make you feel inferior without your permission" is worth bearing in mind. You might also want to consider the following dos and don'ts before your next family gathering:

Do:

➤ Encourage your spouse to take part in some of the difficult conversations with his or her parents. Try to present a united front: "Ann and I don't allow the children to play with toy guns. Would you mind if we exchanged those?"

➤ Talk with your parent-in-law occasionally without your spouse around, as if you were simply two people enjoying a conversation. Ask for advice once in a while.

➤ Find something positive to say whenever possible, especially about your spouse. This is one way of complimenting your in-laws.

Don't:

➤ Call on your in-laws only when you need something (like baby-sitting) from them.

➤ Speak negatively about your in-laws in front of your children.

➤ Use your spouse or your children to carry messages to your own parent or your parent-in-law.

In-laws are a combination of friends you didn't pick out and relatives you only just met. Either way, they've come to stay. Civilized conversation will help you keep everybody connected and let you function as a family.

How to Talk with Much Older People

I've looked at life from both sides now.
—Joni Mitchell, "Both Sides Now," 1967

When you talk to someone even older than your parents' generation, meet them halfway. Whether you are a teenager who is experiencing too many changes or an adult who is bearing too many responsibilities, talking to people who are older than you can give you a larger perspective. They've been where you are. The world may seem different now, but much is still the same. Get them talking about their interests. Don't underestimate them yourself, and don't let them off the hook if they downplay their own strengths.

When you talk with older people, avoid questions that might suggest they are valued less because they are old. Surely a question with the underlying meaning "Are *you* still here?" would be disheartening for anyone, especially a person who has recently retired or is beginning to have health problems. Ageism—like any -ism—drains the life out of civilized conversation in two ways: it shows that you don't value them, and it leaves them with no possible way to give a polite response.

AWFUL: *Are you doing anything nowadays? What were you?*

BARELY CIVIL: *Are you still working? Tell me what you used to do.*

CIVILIZED: *The last time we talked, you were working as a consultant part-time, getting into gardening, and traveling.*

MOST CIVILIZED: *What's new on the consulting front? What have you learned from gardening?*

You can approach much older people with courtesy if you:

Do:

➤ Explore topics (movies, books, travels, hobbies, and family) that will allow them to share their perspective in a way that will broaden yours.

➤ Ask questions about what it was like when they were your age or at your life stage.

➤ Talk about the aging process itself if they seem interested and willing. Ask about their experience of retirement, a move to a different home, even philosophical ideas.

➤ Use conventional etiquette. Address them by Mr., Mrs., or Dr.

➤ Speak clearly! Many older adults are hard of hearing.

Don't:

➤ Start out by calling them by their first names.

➤ Trivialize an older person's "outdated" ideas.

➤ Mumble, use slang, or swear.

How to Talk with Older Adults Who Have Memory Loss

It's a poor sort of memory that only works backwards,
the Queen remarked.

—Lewis Carroll, *Through the Looking Glass and*
  What Alice Found There, 1872

When you talk with an older person who has difficulty with her memory, focus on the person she has become, not the person you have lost. Go where she is, not where reality is. Don't contradict and correct her chronology of events.

A person with an extreme form of memory loss (like the middle stages of Alzheimer's disease) will ask the same questions many times and seem content with the answers every time. Even mild memory loss erases recent memories first, so you may be able to have a pleasant, coherent conversation about the remote past. If you focus on the present, it may help to have a picture or object to talk about. Reintroduce yourself cheerfully every time you encounter each other and every time the conversation circles back to the beginning.

If you limit your encounters to people who are just like you, you will circumscribe your potential of who you can be and harden your sense of self into an us-against-them mentality. You also will not know what to do someday when you become them. You risk missing out on what an older person can offer you—a road map of where you're heading—as well as what a younger person evokes—a memory of the places you've been.

Conversations Between Men and Women

Think of what I'm saying, we can work it out
And get it straight or say good night.
—Paul McCartney, "We Can Work It Out," 1965

E VEN PEOPLE who talk easily across differences of age, job, and culture may find that gender separates them. Sometimes men and women feel that talking to each other is like visiting a different country—or a different planet. It is more helpful to think of what they say as two maps of the same territory. Though they may have the same things to say about their lives, they have different ground rules for what to talk about, and why, and how.

You can have more fun talking if you make allowances for these differences of topic, expectation, and technique.

Topics of Conversation: His, Hers, Theirs

"Sex, gizmos, food, beer, cars"
  —*Maxim* magazine cover banner

"50 ways to have fun with your man!"
  —*Cosmopolitan* magazine cover story

"How to plan for your retirement"
  —*Newsweek* magazine cover story

Until recently, men and women inhabited separate conversational spheres that rarely overlapped. Men were the prime movers in war, sports, academics, politics, and the professions, while women controlled the home, children, primary education, meals, clothes, and socializing. Because of this segregation into two worlds, they did not have as many topics in common when they met and conversed as men and women have today. In fact, most of their social conversation went on in single-sex groups. In some traditional societies, the women had their own living quarters and even their own language.

While much of this segregation by gender has changed, a quick glance at any magazine stand will confirm that many stereotypes remain. These assumptions find their way into conversations between men and women. A young woman lawyer, married to another lawyer, recently told me, "I've noticed that when we go to meetings out of town, people ask me 'Who's looking after the kids?' while they ask Keith 'How's the family?' I grit my teeth and remind myself that they're not necessarily trying to imply that he's the head of the family and I'm the nanny. They are probably just curious how a two-career family covers all the contingencies—but they ought to realize how revealing this kind of question is."

While you are searching for topics to talk about with someone of the opposite sex, you don't want to offend the other person by stereotyping him as being interested only in "men's" topics or her as being interested only in "women's" topics. Thus, to get a conversation going, you have to either stick to areas of common human interest (like family, work, or travel) or work a little harder to find special interests that you both happen to share or know about secondhand.

Avoid gaffes like the one made by a very self-important guy at a dinner party, who turned to the woman seated next to him and asked, "Whose wife are you?" If you've been judging people by their appearance, your shallowness may trip you up and make you miss the conversations that could add more depth to your life.

Two Views of One Conversation

In addition to choosing different topics to talk about, sometimes men and women approach the same conversation from separate angles and in retrospect view it through a different lens. The man may see the conversation as a chance to get his opinion heard, while the woman may be trying to reconcile their differences. Or a woman may avoid hurting a man's feelings by not contradicting him, while the man pays her the compliment of telling her what he sees as the truth.

Sociologists have observed that in conversation, women manage the relationship, whereas men manage what is being talked about. In other words, women see conversation as a road-building process and men are more concerned with the traffic along the road. Men and women also tend to come away from conversations with widely differing interpretations of the messages that were exchanged. While men may be content with "just the facts, ma'am," women may spend more time considering how the information relates to who they are.

Two Sets of Tools

Men listen to women less frequently than women listen to men, because the act of listening has different meanings for them. Some men really don't want to listen at length because they feel it frames them as subordinate. Many women do want to listen, but they expect it to be reciprocal.

—Deborah Tannen, *You Just Don't Understand*, 1990

Even when men and women share topics of interest and understand each other's perspectives, they still may find that they talk and listen using different ground rules. Linguistics expert Deborah Tannen calls these two gender-specific styles "rapport-talk" and "report talk." She asserts that women seek approval (Do you like me?) while men seek respect (Do you respect me?). A woman more often invites others to speak and waits to be invited to speak; a man assumes that what he says is interesting and that others will seize an opening if they want to talk.

Also, when social scientists analyze men and women in conversation, certain patterns emerge. Although both sexes react the same way to interruptions and interrupters, men tend to interrupt more and they interrupt others sooner than women do. Women have greater reluctance to take charge and change the subject. They apologize for things that men either do not acknowledge or that they pin on others. For instance, many people notice that if a telephone conversation is cut off, women will apologize for their own phone service, whereas men blame the problem on the connection or the other phone.

Even the mechanics of body language is tied to gender. Women speaking with women spend much more time looking at each other than men do when they speak to other men. As part of their more conciliatory, approval-seeking style, women tend to touch the other person more often, while men break off eye contact more frequently and stand side by side or at right angles, rather than facing each other to talk.

In spite of these differences, men and women can choose from among many avenues when they talk. There's no reason to pigeonhole each other or to limit what they can learn from each other. They may even discover that they have something in common. While they bring their own perspectives and styles to the discussion, both women and men enjoy talking about sports, the arts, politics, families, food, drink, feelings, and ideas—in short, the things that make life rich and fun.

Romantic or Platonic?

Especially, do not feign affection.
—Max Ehrmann, *Desiderata*, 1927

I need to have loved you; I need to have told you so.
—James Dickey, "A Kindness," 1974

Although on the surface they may appear to be talking about problems with the boss, dog training, or movie reviews, conversations between men and women can also carry the unspoken question of romantic involvement. This search for love is the eternally fascinating subject of thousands of the world's greatest plays, novels, and songs, and the foundation of many industries from fashion to film.

Every field of scientific study has a different view of what's going on when men and women talk around the topic of falling in love. Anthropology catalogs the variety of customs and taboos; zoology studies the conversation as a kind of mating dance; game theory analyzes the mathematical matrix that governs how people try to optimize the outcome; and psychology looks at why people say what they say (and hide what they hide).

Among the scientists who study the phenomenon of flirting, sociologists and linguists focus on what's being transacted. Of course, most spoken conversations don't touch the topic. Sometimes one person is treating the conversation as a flirtation while the other is simply ordering a large pepperoni pizza. But once in a while, people begin to pick up each other's key words and gestures. When this happens, two questions emerge: "Are we talking about romance here?" and "If we are, are you interested in me and am I interested in you?"

Sometimes the setting lends some clarity. Romantic involvement is less likely to be the subtext of an encounter in an elevator than it is at a cocktail party. It's easier to be platonic than romantic at work; just the opposite is true at a singles' bar. Take care not to abuse your setting by talking about office business with a single guy who is mainly looking for a date or flirting with a coworker who not only can't, but mustn't, get involved. The situation can also interfere with the game itself—it's hard to flirt with other people listening in, or when you're under emotional stress, or when you're rushed, or when there's competition.

Most married people leave this gamble alone. They rely on the ring, the baby stroller, or their better half standing guard nearby to ensure that they don't appear to be available. You can usually identify those who pretend to be unattached by their key phrases: "My wife doesn't understand me," "My husband isn't possessive," "We're going to get divorced soon," or "Husband? What husband?"

Single people have to make more choices in order to keep the conversation civilized. When a young woman meets a man whom she finds interesting, all at once she has to determine whether: this conversation is indeed about availability (Is he married/taken?); he is *interested* enough to make the pursuit worthwhile (Does he seem to like me?); and he is *interesting* enough for her to continue (Do I like him?). If the answer to any of these questions is no, she has to communicate tactfully that "this conversation is not about romance"—either to save face herself or to avoid leading him on. He, of course, is doing the same thing.

We might streamline this complicated process by simply making all available people show up at the same spot, pair off, ask each other these yes/no questions, match answers, and then go off to the chapel or back to the crowd to pair off again. That's engineering. Conversation is an art, however, and the real art in flirting is to accomplish all this without acknowledging that it is happening at all.

Buddy or Beloved, the Discovery Process

A beginning is the time for taking the most delicate care that the balances are correct.
—Frank Herbert, *Dune*, 1965

While you're getting to know an acquaintance well enough to decide if you are interested romantically, be courteous and humane. Don't job-interview him on the spot with questions that reveal your desperation for love and your tunnel vision about pursuing it. Don't immediately drop him if he gets one answer "wrong." People are still people outside of your romantic use for them. Keep your flirting civilized by asking fair questions:

- **MORE CIVILIZED:** "Do you have family nearby?"

  LESS CIVILIZED: "Are you married or single?"

- **MORE CIVILIZED:** "What do you do with your free time? (Parents don't have free time, and married people have to check with their spouses.)

  LESS CIVILIZED: "Do you want to get lucky?"

- **MORE CIVILIZED:** "Can I see you sometime?"

  LESS CIVILIZED: "Will you go out with me?"

Don't issue, or accept, invitations into intimate situations without being prepared to deal with their related expectations. Invitations are symbolic. An invitation to dinner is a declaration of interest, doubly so if it is at your house, triply so if it is just the two of you. Lunch can go either way. A breakfast invitation is a low-investment, low-yield strategy, and coffee is about as non-committal as it gets.

Advice books on how to seduce the opposite sex don't always apply to you. You can spice up what you say, but don't try to pose as someone you aren't. For instance, in *Double Your Dating,* David DeAngelo cautions men who are meeting women to avoid the mention of "chess, computers, comic books, Star Wars [and] monster trucks" or "topics that will make you look like the biggest loser alive." To some women, however, these topics would make you a winner!

If you ask "Do you have a card?" you can keep up the fiction that your interest is businesslike and aboveboard; if you say "Would you give me your phone number?" you imply that none of that matters as much as just being able to see her again. If you help her on with her coat at the end of an otherwise singles-only evening, you've sent a signal that you have nice manners and you want her to notice, all without committing yourself.

IF YOUR TALK WITH THE OPPOSITE SEX chronically leads to places you'd rather not go, remind yourself that you have some control over the outcome. Whether it's a yes or a no you're looking for, if you're not getting it, you can review and change your strategies. Don't expect indiscriminate flirting to retain its value if people figure out it's all just an act. Don't keep acting like a pal if you want to show your crush you'd like to be more than friends. If you keep doing what you're doing, you'll keep getting what you're getting. If you look with detachment at your own conversation, you can change whatever it is that doesn't contribute to the result you want.

◦ ◦ ◦

The People You Meet: The Chronic Flirt

Sometimes you may meet a person who just can't seem to help himself; he flirts shamelessly. It may be the only way he knows how to relate to the opposite gender. Conversations always seem to return to discussions of looks or are infused with sexual innuendo. If he is married, his wife may be aware of his conversational style and either watches him like a hawk or lets him have his harmless fun.

In general, women seem more aware of how to keep a conversation "on track." If you want to block or slow down a flirtation, use "I" a lot, "you" a little, and "we" never. You can also use discouraging body language—offering less eye contact, turning slightly away from facing the man, expanding the distance between you. To nip a romance in the bud, dispense with the doe-eyed admiration of what he says and instead disagree with him, crack jokes, and invite a third and fourth person into the conversation. Any older man who talks to a younger woman with laborious gallantries rather than genuine conversation can be returned to reality if she calls him "Mr." or "sir" rather than his first name, or gets up and offers him a seat.

If you wish to cool down a conversation that seems to be veering into a romantic flirtation, you should decline an invitation to dinner but say you're available for coffee sometime (if you want to be friends). Be sure to get your signals straight. Don't string someone along or confuse her. Married men should be particularly careful to be clear about their status early in the game and to "do right," as Pearl Buck says, in spite of their feelings.

If you are in a conversation with a chronic flirt, don't overreact. Civilized flirting sometimes reaches an equilibrium. If you flirt in a context in which neither of you intends to take action, then you can have the best of both worlds. History records the contrasting styles of two British prime ministers: dignified, stuffy William Gladstone and courtly, polished Benjamin Disraeli. Queen Victoria, who was middle aged, plump, dowdy, and deeply attached to her dead husband, pronounced disapprovingly of Gladstone, "He speaks to me as if I was a public meeting." In contrast, she reveled in Disraeli's elaborate flirtation while she understood it for what it was: "Mr. Gladstone makes me feel that he is the most brilliant person in the kingdom; Mr. Disraeli makes me feel that I am."

Keep Talking

Attention is a silent and perpetual flattery.
—Madame Swetchine, *Life and Letters of Madame Swetchine*, 1868

Civilized conversations between individuals in a long-term twosome can create a safe oasis in social situations. To keep this oasis green, always support each other and help each other look and sound good in public. Don't undermine each other. Don't promote the cliché of the bickering old married couple who continually point out each other's foibles or rehash old arguments. Don't openly contradict or squabble; it makes people uncomfortable.

Beyond personal comments, don't issue generalizations about the sexes when your better half is the implied sample you are generalizing from. Economist John Stuart Mill said sagely, "You can tell a lot about a man's wife by hearing his opinions about women in general." Do your spouse a favor; get off that soapbox.

While you are keeping conversation clear of criticism about your partner and his kind, don't go overboard in the other direction and have eyes and ears only for each other in a crowd. Don't talk only to each other or exclude others by reverting to private injokes. Don't indulge in a pas de deux in front of other people. My family used to refer to some acquaintances as the "he him" couple because she would stand next to her husband at a party and talk about what he was thinking or what he would say—as if he weren't standing right there.

AS THE FRENCH, those champions of both talk and romance, put it: *"Vive la difference!"* No matter which planet they come from, and whether they are looking for friendship, romance, or long-term amity, men and women can bridge the gender gap to discover what they have to say to each other. Good conversation will improve the quality of their connection as fellow human beings.

· VIII ·

Conversations with All Kinds of People

Everyone Is Someone

—Book title, Doris G. Monteux, 1962

GOOD CONVERSATION can reach across age and gender differences to connect people. With only a small extra effort, it can also bridge the gulfs created when one person speaks a different language or has a physical, mental, or social difficulty. This chapter includes tips on how to have a successful conversation despite these obstacles and how to put others at ease if you are the one who can't hear, see, or speak clearly.

How to Talk with People Who Speak a Different Language

When you strike up a conversation with someone whose first language is not English, immediately try to gauge his level of fluency. Even the most fluent speaker of English may not pick up subtle allusions, slang, cutting-edge jargon, or shoptalk if English is not his native tongue.

One of my children was adopted from Korea at age three, and he had to pick up English in a hurry. We were mystified by his greeting—"Wayjeedunn?"—until we realized that he was repeating our own slovenly rendering of "What ya doin'?"

Clarify both your vocabulary and the delivery of your words when you talk with intermediate English speakers. Researchers at MIT have begun to explore "clear speech" to improve conversations with both non-native English speakers and people who are deaf. Clear speech has four distinct elements:

1. Simplify the words you use, and enunciate clearly ("yes" instead of "yeah").

2. Speak a little slower than usual.

3. Pause slightly between words and sentences ("What's up?" rather than " 's'up?").

4. Speak just a little louder than usual.

In addition to being mindful of how you speak, consider the ways in which non-native speakers of English may misinterpret your use of acronyms. One visitor from England was aghast to hear her coworker discuss putting money into her IRA—she thought this meant Americans had an official way to subsidize the Irish Republican Army!

As you speak with a person who may have trouble understanding your language,

Do:

➤ Make eye contact.

➤ Use body language and gestures.

➤ Ask simple questions. (Many people find it easier to speak a second language than to listen and understand it.)

➤ Provide props—a picture, object, or meal.

➤ Wait for signs of understanding or incomprehension.

Don't:

➤ Change the topic abruptly.

➤ Shout or mumble.

➤ Be vague or use slang.

➤ Talk to or ask questions of a translator. Keep your attention on the other person and just look pleasant while your words are being respoken.

If you are the not-too-fluent speaker of a foreign language, limit your conversation to simple specifics. Chitchat, hypothetical ideas, discussions of past and future events, wit, puns, and abstractions can take you out of your depth. Also,

Do:

➤ Make it clear to the other person when you cannot comprehend everything he says.

➤ Show respect to other people by trying the phrases in their language that you know. Don't assume everyone wants to speak English. On the other hand, don't insist on limping along in their language if they can speak yours better.

➤ Try to speak with three or four people at a time so that you can listen to them talk to one another three-fourths of the time.

If you are speaking a foreign language, anticipate settings where you will need to talk, and practice a few answers to routine questions so you don't feel completely at a loss.

When I spent a summer in Lima, Peru, I had to learn Spanish quickly. I memorized sentences to describe my name, my age and situation, where I lived, how long I had been there, and how much I enjoyed Lima. Those lines, plus a cheat sheet by the telephone to help me deal with wrong numbers (my own and others'), launched me into the deep end of the conversational swim, where I could learn by social immersion.

When you find yourself outnumbered by people who speak another language and you need to take a rest from constant mental translation, you can say something you've memorized beforehand for just this purpose: "I can't keep up—I think I'll just enjoy listening for a while."

When Physical Difficulties Interfere with Conversation

Creative courtesy can help two people compensate for uneven proficiency in a language they are using to communicate with each other. Courtesy can also bridge the gap created by many disabilities that make speech and hearing difficult.

When you are speaking with someone who has a physical problem, always let him decide whether to discuss the condition or just converse without mentioning it. Try to squelch your own curiosity or prejudice. Be attuned to the ways in which you can minimize the effect of his disability so that you can simply get to know each other and enjoy each other's company.

Blindness

Conversing with a blind person can be disconcerting at first because sighted people sometimes make unwarranted assumptions about blind people's capabilities, and blind people rely on clues other than eye contact to pace the conversation. Both of these deficits can be offset by courtesy and understanding on both sides.

To compensate for his lack of visual contact, you can be sensitive to his other facial and body cues and to the tone of voice that he uses to suggest when to speak, when to listen, and when the topic is going to shift. Imagine that you are talking on the phone, and try to make up for the absence of visual clues.

Provide clues about what is going on around him, just out of earshot. If you haven't been introduced, be sure he knows that you are standing nearby and say who you are. Then let him know when someone is about to join the conversation and monitor what is going on in the larger group.

Don't shout out directions to a blind person who is trying to get oriented ("Go left," "I'm over here"). Instead, ask him if he would like to take your arm, and don't insist if he declines.

Deafness

Mild or severe deafness need not prevent good conversation if both parties are aware of the problem and work together to keep the dialog moving along. Be considerate, especially to older people who may be hard of hearing and to those who clearly wear a hearing aid, get lost in the conversation, ask "What?" repeatedly, or cup a hand to the ear.

People who have trouble hearing may prefer to talk a lot because then at least they know what the conversation is about. They may jump in and change the topic abruptly because they have no idea what is being said or that other conversations are already going on. In one-to-one conversation, they may miss auditory clues, such as the breath that a person takes in or slight throat clearing before she begins to speak; without such clues, a person who is deaf may start "talking over" the other person. Deaf people also tend to frown in concentration when they are trying to hear and speak too loudly because they cannot gauge the level of their own voices. Be understanding about the conversational awkwardness that sometimes results.

Some deaf people purposely avoid large gatherings because it is too hard to follow a group conversation; sometimes you'll need to make a special effort to converse with them one to one. To compensate for this difficulty, you also can pay attention to conversational settings. Avoid large, open, and noisy places like restaurants. If you must meet in this type of setting, tone down background noise or ask the manager to turn down the music in a restaurant.

The same techniques of "clear speech" that make English more accessible to the non-native speaker (enunciate clearly; slow down; lengthen pauses between words; and speak up without shouting) can also help people who have trouble hearing.

In addition to speaking clearly, maintain the courtesies of ordinary speech.

Do:

➤ Face the person.

➤ Get her attention./Maintain eye contact.

➤ Look at her while you speak. Let her see your lips form the words.

➤ Start with a familiar topic and don't change it abruptly.

➤ If she is deaf in one ear, find out which side is her "good side."

➤ Mention distractions (inaudible to her) that may take your attention away from the conversation: "Another guest has rung the doorbell."

➤ Be her "ear to the ground" about what is happening in the larger group and other conversations nearby.

Don't:

➤ Shout or mumble.

➤ Give up and say "Never mind" or "It's not important." Instead, say "I'll explain it later when it's not so noisy."

➤ Make annoyed comments in a low voice. Hearing loss is patchy, and you may be overheard.

If you are hard of hearing or deaf, help people out. For example, you might say:

➤ I'm having trouble hearing. May I talk with you away from the TV?

➤ I'm sorry, but I can't hear you over the music. Can we continue this conversation later?

➤ Could I sit on your left? My right ear is better.

➤ I would love to hear what you are talking about. Would you fill me in when the noise goes down a little?

You may need to seek quieter settings within large social gatherings. Fair or not, the same people who are happy to bellow at you one on one don't always like to shout at each other in a group so you can listen in. Let people know your difficulty, assure them that you would love to talk with them, and wait until the conversation splits up into smaller groups.

Being in a Wheelchair

Many fascinating people are left out of conversations simply because their wheelchairs keep them two feet below the level of talk. Nancy Mairs, author of *Waist-High in the World: A Life among the Nondisabled,* says, "For God's sake, sit down." If you expect a conversation with a wheelchair user to last longer than a minute, find somewhere to sit down or squat down to her eye level. Doing so shows respect and can ease the strain on her neck. A few adjustments to your attitude can also compensate for her lack of altitude:

> ➤ Treat her with grown-up good manners. Shake hands. Make eye contact.

> ➤ Don't violate her personal space by touching or moving her chair unless you ask first.

> ➤ Say truthfully how you are doing. Don't let guilt over your relative mobility lead you to focus on some other complaint to balance your luck.

If your child blurts out a blunt question or rude remark ("That man has no legs!"), use it as a "teachable moment"—don't shush her. Explain the facts pleasantly: he cannot walk, so he uses a wheelchair to get around. Say that you don't know why he can't walk. You might make eye contact with him and see if the lesson can include an introduction and more explanation. Most wheelchair users would prefer this kind of matter-of-factness to being the object of pity or pained squeamishness.

Speech Difficulties

Aside from blindness, deafness, and "seated-ness," all of which can interfere with the various mechanics of conversation, speech difficulties can hinder a speaker's pronunciation. Many congenital conditions can make speech challenging; these include stuttering, cleft lip and palate, and deafness. Problems that occur later in life like stroke and head injuries, types of cancers that lead to removal of the larynx, multiple sclerosis, and Parkinson's disease also can alter a person's speech.

In general, even though someone may be struggling to get words out, don't make that struggle the topic of conversation. The only thing that sometimes excuses you from this taboo is full or associate membership in his club—if you have the same condition or a very close relative does. Even then, don't bring up the speech difficulty until later in the conversation, and don't try to one-up the listener or compare your woes. Just ask for his ideas, try to see the situation through his eyes, and show that you are seeing a person, not a diagnosis.

Don't assume that because conversation may be difficult, it is unwelcome. On the contrary, conversation may be one of the few things that can help someone who is struggling. "Patients say the most frustrating symptom of Parkinson's disease is losing their ability to communicate through normal speech," says Joseph P. Atkins, MD, chief of otorhinolaryngology and head and neck surgery at Pennsylvania Hospital. A simple conversation can celebrate who a person is rather than what he lacks.

A person who stutters may do so more because of the pressure of noisy social situations, encounters with strangers, and conversations with a person who seems bothered by her unclear speech. Engineer Bob Lauer writes: "I do still stutter—depending on who

I'm talking with, the circumstances, what side of the bed I got up on that morning, and the state of my love life. It's not a big issue for me, if people could just not focus on it."

When you speak with someone who stutters, maintain eye contact while she searches for the right sound to get past a stumbling block. Although it's tempting to step in and supply the word that she seems to be looking for, wait for her to say it. Also,

Do:

➤ Try to pause a second or so before you fire an answer right back or counter with your own question. This will help make talking less hurried, more relaxed.

➤ Try not to be upset or annoyed if her stuttering increases.

➤ Say to a child who stutters, "It's okay," "Take your time," "It's hard to talk sometimes," and "Lots of people get stuck."

Don't:

➤ Focus on or get tripped up by the other person's stuttering.

➤ Finish her sentences.

➤ Converse on the telephone if you can possibly talk in person or by e-mail. Telephone conversations tend to be more difficult for people who stutter.

WHEN YOU TALK with a person who cannot speak clearly for other reasons, do not be disconcerted by what's missing (eye contact, verbs, nouns, facial mobility, or motor control). Instead, explore and concentrate on what the person *can* do. If he has had a stroke or head injury, talk to and engage him using touch, objects, pictures, and music.

Multiple sclerosis can leave a person's intellect intact while it causes fatigue and loss of motor control. A person with MS loses fluency and has slowed speech, lower volume, and difficulty finding the right words in conversation. Sometimes he cannot understand what you say. Don't misjudge his slurred speech and diminished motor control as the behaviors of a drunk. Call on your good manners to forge ahead as if he had his original voice tone. Make normal eye contact and slow down—don't chatter awkwardly.

Parkinson's disease can cause a loss of facial mobility that renders a person's face expressionless while he talks. Without a facial expression to respond to, it's easy to reflect a blank face back when you talk to him. Remind yourself to be expressive.

Often the hands of a person with this disease tremble, and he may pause midsentence for a few seconds and then continue without loss of meaning. Medication for this illness may make these gaps in conversation longer and more frequent. Michael McCurdy, a prolific book illustrator coping with Parkinson's, describes his condition this way:

> It takes me some seconds to decide what to say, to wait, and then to take a chance by mumbling something. Of course, it isn't heard well, and people ask, "What?" which only makes me feel more on the spot and more tongue-tied. It's best for people to simply wait quietly till the words come out.

Be patient and relaxed while a person with this disease pauses. Don't jump in and complete his sentences. Though his symptoms get worse over time, his mind will remain as sharp as ever.

Conversations with All Kinds of Minds

Just as your conversations can rise above physical disabilities, you also can have great talks with people who think differently. Watch for simple clues to neurological problems, such as impassive affect, fidgeting, odd speech patterns, and shifting eye contact. As you get acquainted, if you find that the other person doesn't connect in the way you are used to connecting, don't give up. Don't start out by asking "Is something wrong?" Respect the person's dignity.

Attention Deficit Disorder

People with attention deficit disorder (ADD) or attention deficit hyperactivity disorder (ADHD) may interrupt frequently, change the subject, and get distracted easily.

Try to keep the conversation floating along, and bring it back to the main topic occasionally. Don't overreact to flights of fancy or pursue every new tangent. Keep the brakes on. Inattention is how he copes with too much input. Don't be insulted if someone you meet at a party loses focus on your conversation and picks up a magazine a few minutes into your first conversation. He may just be temporarily dealing with sensory overload, and eventually he'll drift right back. Give him the benefit of the doubt. Often the thing that can make a person difficult to talk to can make him especially interesting.

Tourette's Syndrome

A person with Tourette's syndrome may have vocal and/or motor twitches. While you talk, he may shift his fingers, shoulders, or eyelids, hum, or clear his throat repeatedly. (Severe Tourette's also includes jumping, flailing, using off-color language, and calling out.) In fact, the mild tics can be suppressed with effort; if a person is ticking, it means he has relaxed a bit and is following you just fine. Nevertheless, don't expect a person to stop: tics are as irrepressible as sneezes. Keep your composure and carry on with your conversation.

Autism and Asperger's Syndrome

I think in pictures. Words are like a second language to me.

—Temple Grandin, *Thinking in Pictures: And Other Reports from My Life with Autism,* 1995

Autism may present itself starkly, as the antithesis of communication: absence of eye contact, aversion to being touched, lack of affect, and discomfort in social situations. People with autism may have difficulty with the usual forms of verbal and nonverbal communication, especially with interpreting another person's tone of voice, facial expression, and body language.

When you talk with someone who has autism, speak clearly and proceed carefully with simple, closed-ended questions and answers. For instance: "Hello, I like your red sweater. Where did you buy it?" is better than a general "Hi, how are you?" Keep the tone and volume of your voice even; don't shout. Look to the person's parent or caregiver for guidance about how to talk with him.

A person with Asperger's syndrome, a milder form of autism, may make blunt comments or all-too-personal disclosures. As the parent of one child with Asperger's noted, "It's like he's got the words but not the music." His speech may be mechanically abbreviated so that he omits all "padding" words not essential to the meaning of a sentence.

When you talk with him, don't try for subtle humor, banter, or small talk. Don't hop from subject to subject. If he talks obsessively about one subject, don't try to talk about something else. You can join him in conversation if you take an interest in what he cares about.

While everyone struggles to master the civilities of conversation, Asperger's can keep a person from understanding them at all. The most important conversational skill you can contribute is not to take his underdeveloped social skills personally. Instead, appreciate him for his often highly intelligent ideas, for his aspirations, for his unvarnished honesty, and for the attachments he inspires in others.

You may surmise, but not know for sure, that a person has a condition like Asperger's. Before you dismiss a person as being doleful, quirky, awkward, or rude, consider the fact that his or her behavior may have an underlying explanation. Then proceed with respect.

Difficulties in talking and listening should not keep you from good conversation; you can reach across them to connect with anyone you encounter. People are more, much more, than what holds them back. Legs or eardrums, voice boxes or retinas, or physical prowess do not make the difference. If your heart is in the right place, that's the only body part that matters.

· IX ·

Conversations on the Telephone, over the Internet, and on Paper

Don't write anything that you can phone, don't phone anything
that you can talk face to face, don't talk anything face to face
that you can smile, don't smile anything that you can wink, and
don't wink anything that you can nod.

—Attributed to Earl Long, Louisiana politician, 1895–1960

EOPLE CAN BENEFIT from good conversation not just when they speak in person, but also when they talk over the telephone, type on the Internet, and handwrite on paper. A few tips will help you add human depth to these otherwise two-dimensional conversations so that the warmth of personal contact isn't chilled by the mechanics of the technology.

Conversations on the Telephone

When at last this little instrument appeared, consisting, as it does, of parts every one of which is familiar to us, and capable of being put together by an amateur, the disappointment arising from its humble appearance was only partially relieved on finding that it was really able to talk.

—James Clerk Maxwell, *The Telephone*, 1878

The telephone cuts away the visual dimension of a conversation, forcing people to rely on the voice alone without the added intimations of facial expressions and body language.

Be courteous and identify yourself to whoever answers. Don't make the answerer guess who you are. My daughters sound like each other when they start out "It's me, Mom," and they are amazed if I misidentify them. If you don't say who you are, you give up your right to be offended, and you just slow down the start of the conversation.

Say briefly why you are calling without too much beating around the small-talk bush. Make it clear if you just need a quick answer to a question or if you want to catch up at leisure. Ask "Is now a good time to talk?" or "Do you have a few minutes?" to be sure you are not interrupting a meal, another conversation, another phone call, or a project.

When to Take a Stand and When to Take a Seat

➤ If you plan to talk at length on the telephone with a close acquaintance, relax. Sit down or even lie down.

➤ If you have ordinary business to transact, sit at a desk.

➤ If you want to project confidence on a business call, stand up. Your voice will "stand up" too.

➤ If you want to keep a conversation very short, stand up the whole time.

If other people can overhear you where you are phoning (especially if you are on a cell phone), move away, turn your back, and lower your voice out of courtesy to those around you and for the privacy of the person on the phone. Never talk on the phone in the midst of a group, as if a person not present is more important than those who are.

Consider the possibility that the other person is not alone in the room (her end of the conversation may be overheard) or is on a speakerphone (the whole conversation may be overheard). She also may be distracted with another activity. If you hear water running, children screaming, or keyboard keys clacking, you may have called at a time when the speaker can't give you her full attention.

Keep cell phone calls on public transportation short. Three-quarters of all cell phone conversations are not very interesting, even to the participants: a quarter are basically "I'm getting on the bus, I'm on the bus, I'm getting off the bus" or "I'm running late." Another quarter are "Can you hear me now?" or "You're breaking up." The third quarter are mind-numbing, like "Do you want 2 percent or skim?" or stomach-turning, like "Let me tell you what the doctor said about my yeast infection." Precious few cell phoners let the eavesdroppers go home with a good anecdote to make up for being forced to listen. Don't conduct intimate conversations in public earshot; not only does it make people hear things they'd rather not, but it keeps them from enjoying their own live conversations with each other.

Speakerphones

Bridget Jones: It's me. Just wondered how you are.

Mark Darcy: I'm fine thanks. Everything all right with you?

Bridget Jones: Fine, though, er, I've just had a rather graphic shag flashback. You do have a genuinely gorgeous bottom.

Mark Darcy: Right, well, thank you. I'm actually with the Mexican Ambassador just at the moment and the Head of Amnesty International and the Under Secretary for Trade and Industry and you're on speakerphone.

—From the film *Bridget Jones: The Edge of Reason,* 2004

Inform the other person if she is on a speakerphone, and name who is listening in. Use speakers only when more than one person needs to listen together. Don't do one-on-one, personal conversations on speakers unless you must—it is rude in its implication that you are doing something else with your hands, and can be embarrassing if anyone overhears a private conversation. Headsets are a much better way to keep your hands free and your conversation semiprivate.

Conversations Online

E-mail is often a good substitute for a utilitarian telephone call, condensing simple information into a message that would otherwise intrude as a phone call and take minutes of trivialities to pad it. E-mail erases the problem of time zones; you write in your daytime to someone on the other side of the world and she answers it hours later, in her daytime. It also provides a record of scheduling and wording and keeps people updated on a group project or a scheduled event.

Do:

➤ Check your e-mail regularly, and answer it promptly.

➤ Keep your messages short, simple, and upbeat.

➤ Put a succinct title and your name in the subject box, especially if your e-mail address does not contain your name or if the person does not know you well. People who are cautious will just delete your message without opening it.

➤ Start with a salutation including the recipient's name, and sign off with yours, unless the message is very short, like "Make it 12:30 instead."

Don't:

➤ Trust your e-mail pals with gossip, complaints, or sensitive financial information. If you just have to let your conversation go slumming in the gossip ghetto, do it in person, one-on-one, face-to-face, without a record.

➤ Get too romantic in print during the early stages of a relationship, *especially* if there is a third party to be hurt, unless you trust the dear one to keep the messages private and delete them if the relationship ends.

➤ Type messages in all capitals. Called "flaming," IT IS THE EQUIVALENT OF SHOUTING IN PERSON. If you want to emphasize words, put *asterisks* before and after to draw attention.

➤ E-mail "everyone" the latest petition, joke, or hot news item. It's easy for you, but it feels like spam after a while. I have occasionally asked someone who should know better to stop joke-spamming or daily-blogging me on his "everybody" list.

➢ Write a long e-mail without occasionally acknowledging your reader with "As you know . . ." or "I wanted to ask you." That puts her in the conversation, rather than just making her the audience for your monologue.

When a Conversation Is Better on Paper

If you are happy, do not promise anything.
If you are angry, do not mail a letter.
—Confucius, 551–479 BC

While you augment and reinforce your conversational life on line, don't forget the traditional medium of pen and ink. Some things still sound better when you say them on paper. You choose better words with a pen in your hand, the person pays more attention to them because you put extra effort in on them, and you can convey your personality through your taste in paper, color, stamp, and handwriting.

Even the most civilized conversation is not the best way to let some of your feelings be known. *Praise* and *thanks,* delightful as they are to hear in person, are twice as nice if they are handwritten in a letter or note that the person can read and reread. When you unwrap a gift and the person who gave it is not there, send a thank-you note immediately. Write your thanks by mail even when you've already said thank you out loud. *Condolence* for a death or loss is also extra comforting on paper. Many bereaved people describe themselves later as having passed the first weeks in a merciful blur, so a letter will comfort them at their own pace, whenever they are ready. An *apology* is often easier to make on paper. You may want to deliver it personally with a short, spoken apology as you hand it over. When you want to give people time to think over your words, a written *request for help* allows the other person to take time to consider his answer, and a written *invitation* sets the mood for a special occasion while it lets the person check her schedule before saying yes. Use your mind's ear to take what you would have said out loud and dress up those words with your own handwriting.

The exceptions to the rule that "paper is better" are urgent information, legally binding admissions, and angry complaints. (Don't write "I need to know immediately," "I accept legal liability," or "I'm mad at you.") If you have *a complaint, a criticism,* or *bad news,* it's usually best to deliver it face-to-face. When you write down something negative, the person is not there to react to it, so that, getting no reaction, you tend to repeat and intensify it. If you happen to be wrong, it can be very awkward to retract harsh written words. Have the courage to deliver bad news in person—it will soften what you say and how the person reacts.

Don't be seduced by the idea that you can substitute e-mail for the important handwritten messages listed above. They look infinitely more friendly and dignified on paper rather than onscreen, and are well worth the effort. Your words will get extra attention when they arrive under a stamp, on stationery, in your writing. Keep your notepaper, address book, stamps, and a pen near your keyboard so you don't have to go looking for them. These courtesies will repay your trouble many times over. For guidance with this type of communication, see my book *The Art of the Handwritten Note.*

Only Connect

Regardless of the form in which it is conveyed, the art of conversation helps you touch the people in your life. With the right words, you can clarify your own thoughts, express who you are, celebrate small everyday victories, strengthen your relationships, and knit together the community around you. No matter who you are or where you are, every time you talk you have the chance to transform ordinary words into something exceptional. Civilized conversation, like all art, connects you to the best in other people and in yourself.

Bibliography

Augsburger, David. *The New Freedom of Forgiveness.* Chicago: Moody Press, 2000.

Averick, Leah Shifrin. *Don't Call Me Mom: How to Improve Your In-Law Relationships.* Hollywood, FL: Lifetime Books, 1996.

Barash, Susan Shapiro. *Mothers-in-Law and Daughters-in-Law: Love, Hate, Rivalry and Reconciliation.* Far Hills, NJ: New Horizon, 2001.

———. *The New Wife: The Evolving Role of the American Wife.* Lenexa, KS: Nonetheless, 2004.

Bowditch, Eden Unger, and Aviva Samet. *The Daughter-in-Law's Survival Guide: Everything You Need to Know About Relating to Your Mother-in-Law.* Oakland, CA: New Harbinger Publications, 2002.

Elgin, Suzette Haden. *How to Turn the Other Cheek and Still Survive in Today's World.* New York: Thomas Nelson, Inc., 1997.

Engel, Beverly. *The Power of Apology: Healing Steps to Transform All Your Relationships.* New York: John Wiley & Sons, 2001.

Fisher, Roger, William Ury, and Bruce Patton. *Getting to Yes: Negotiating Agreement without Giving In.* New York: Penguin Books, 1991.

Forni, P. M. *Choosing Civility: The Twenty-five Rules of Considerate Conduct.* New York: St. Martin's Griffin, 2002.

Gabor, Don. *How to Start a Conversation and Make Friends.* New York: Simon & Schuster, 1983.

Garner, Alan. *Conversationally Speaking.* Los Angeles: Lowell House, 1997.

Gary, Juneau Mahon, and Linda Remolino. *Coping with Loss and Grief*

Through Online Support Groups. Greensboro, NC: ERIC Clearinghouse on Counseling and Student Services, 2000.

Geertz, Clifford. *Local Knowledge: Further Essays in Interpretive Anthropology.* New York: Basic Books, 1983.

Goffman, Erving. *The Presentation of Self in Everyday Life.* New York: Anchor, 1959.

Guilmartin, Nance. *Healing Conversations: What to Say When You Don't Know What to Say.* San Francisco: Jossey-Bass, 2002.

Hall, Edward T. *The Hidden Dimension.* New York: Doubleday, 1982.

Harris, Thomas. *I'm OK, You're OK.* New York: HarperCollins, 2004.

Hopper, Robert. *Telephone Conversation.* Bloomington: Indiana University Press, 1992.

Ingram, Jay. *Talk, Talk, Talk: Decoding the Mysteries of Speech.* New York: Anchor Books, 1994.

Kano, Susan. *Making Peace with Food: Freeing Yourself from the Diet/Weight Obsession.* New York: Perennial Currents, 1989.

Krause, Jean Christine. "Properties of Naturally Produced Clear Speech at Normal Rates and Implications for Intelligibility Enhancement." Ph.D. diss., Massachusetts Institute of Technology, 2001.

Lerner, Harriet. *The Dance of Anger: A Woman's Guide to Changing the Patterns of Intimate Relationships.* New York: Quill, 1997.

Lewis, Clive Staples. *A Grief Observed.* New York: Harper & Row, 1961.

Locke, John. *Why We Don't Talk to Each Other Anymore: The Devoicing of Society.* New York: Simon & Schuster, 1999.

Mairs, Nancy. *Waist-High in the World: Life Among the Nondisabled.* Boston: Beacon Press, 1996.

Martin, Judith. *The Right Thing to Say (Miss Manners' Basic Training).* New York: Crown, 1998.

Pease, Barbara, and Allan Pease. *Why Men Don't Listen and Women Can't Read Maps: How We're Different and What to Do About It.* New York: Broadway, 1998.

———. *Why Men Don't Have a Clue and Women Always Need More Shoes: The Ultimate Guide to the Opposite Sex.* New York: Broadway, 2004.

Pin, Emile Jean, in collaboration with Jamie Turndorf. *The Pleasure of Your Company: A Socio-Psychological Analysis of Modern Sociability.* Westport, CT: Praeger, 1985.

Roane, Susan. *How to Work a Room: The Ultimate Guide to Savvy Socializing in Person and Online*. New York: HarperResource, 2000.

———. *What Do I Say Next? Talking Your Way to Business and Social Success*. New York: Warner Books, 1997.

Rosen, Mark I., Ph.D. *Thank You for Being Such a Pain: Spiritual Guidance for Dealing with Difficult People*. New York: Three Rivers Press, 1998.

Schiraldi, Glenn R. *The Anger Management Sourcebook*. New York: McGraw-Hill, 2002.

Shepherd, Margaret. *The Art of the Handwritten Note: A Guide to Reclaiming Civilized Conversation*. New York: Broadway Books, 2002.

Skriloff, Lisa, and Jodie Gould. *Men Are from Cyberspace: The Single Woman's Guide to Flirting, Dating, and Finding Love On-Line*. New York: St. Martin's Griffin, 1997.

Tannen, Deborah. *The Argument Culture*. New York: Ballantine, 1998.

———. *I Only Say This Because I Love You: Talking to Your Parents, Partner, Sibs, and Kids When You're All Adults*. New York: Ballantine, 2002.

———. *That's Not What I Meant! How Conversational Style Makes or Breaks Your Relations with Others*. New York: William Morrow and Co., 1986.

———. *You Just Don't Understand: Women and Men in Conversation*. New York: Perennial Currents, 2001.

Trozzi, Maria, and Kathy Massimini. *Talking with Children about Loss: Words, Strategies, and Wisdom to Help Children Cope with Death, Divorce, and Other Difficult Times*. New York: Perigee, 1999.

Zeldin, Theodore. *Conversation*. Mahwah, NJ: Hidden Spring Press, 1998.